Howard's Way

Dhany,
'Best read over a bottle of
Unruly Red.
Enjoy — Hope.

Howard's Way
The First Five Years

Howard Croft

Foreword by Deirdre Buchanan

Howard Croft

RYEDALE
BOOK FESTIVAL

Norton, North Yorkshire

First published in the Great Britain by
Ryedale Book Festival, 2016
www.ryedalebookfestival.com

Copyright © Howard Croft 2016

A catalogue record for this book is available from the British Library

ISBN: 978-0-9935639-0-4

Set and designed in Georgia and American Typewriter fonts by
Helen Lowdell, Malton, North Yorkshire
h.lowdell1@virgin.net

Printed and bound in Great Britain by
Best Print & Design Ltd, Malton, North Yorkshire
www.best-print.co.uk

'Howard's Way' and 'Howard Croft Column' originally published by
Malton and Pickering Mercury
Scarborough, North Yorkshire
www.maltonmercury.co.uk

Dedicated to
Mrs Croft – who else?

And to the memory of
the Reverend Dr Quentin Wilson

Contents

Foreword

The first time I heard talk of Howard's articles in the local press was at a jovial lunch party. Over the roast beef, the talk turned to these literary masterpieces and, I have to admit, I felt sidelined. I was obviously taking the wrong paper. The very next day I telephoned my newsagent and transferred my allegiances to the *Malton and Pickering Mercury*. My weekly copy has dropped on my doormat every Wednesday since and I have not regretted my decision for a moment.

The thing is, having cursorily scanned the headlines, one is drawn inside to find out what is floating Howard's boat each week. The column used to be called *Howard's Way* and a very apt title it was to my way of thinking. However, some whipper-snapper has taken an axe to that tag-line, more's the pity. I would like to see it restored.

That rant aside, you dear reader are now going to have the pleasure of dipping in and out of this admirable book as you please. If you are anything like me, you will chuckle a lot. Howard's articles cover a wide range of subjects, some serious, some comic but they are all so very readable. Here you will find our local council taken to task on various issues, the government too takes some stick but there is always a balance. Howard sees things through the eyes of a man who has experienced much over the years. He has a view that is in tune with the majority of his readers, especially those of us who receive a pension! He also has a ready wit and a wonderful way with words. I am always curious to know what 'Mrs Croft' has been up to. She has been accused of being 'a spender', she is praised for her cooking skills but has a pre-delectation for a frock!

I was very pleased to be asked to write this Foreword for, as I have indicated, there must have been many candidates for the job. I just hope Howard's articles (now syndicated in the more than fifty newspapers and websites of the Johnston Press, including its flagship title *The Yorkshire Post*) continue to flow and that when there are enough of them, there will be a second volume.

In the meantime, I know what my pals will be finding in their Christmas stockings this year.

Deirdre Buchanan
Pickering, Spring 2016

Preface

In 2011 Andrew Pitt, at the time a reporter on the *Malton and Pickering Mercury*, invited me to write a weekly column for his newspaper. Much to my surprise and, I suspect, to his, it attracted quite a following and to our even greater surprise it continued without interruption for several years under the banner *Howard's Way*.

What quickly emerged was a fanciful image of myself as a hapless and curmudgeonly wine bibber of strong opinions, locked in marriage to a difficult and demanding wife, always referred to as "Mrs Croft". The truth is very different: I am a diffident, easy going fellow whose habits can best be described as Methodist, and in real life I always refer to my wife as Fiona.

I have since its inception been a supporter of the Ryedale Book Festival, an unsurprising cause for a retired publisher to embrace, but one to which, as Mrs Croft pointed out, I have contributed little. Why not, she said, publish a collection of your better efforts, even though it might be a very short book, and donate the profits from its sale, if any, to the Book Festival? So, here we are.

I have had a great deal of fun writing my pieces for the *Mercury* and I have been rewarded by countless conversations with readers around the shops in Malton and Norton, and indeed in Pickering and Kirkbymoorside. They usually begin with a shy approach and the words 'Are you the one who writes in the *Mercury*?' I always acknowledge responsibility and ask what they think of it. The responses are not invariably positive. On one hilarious occasion a chap who approached me in the bar at the Wentworth Arms responded 'I think nowt to it. It's bloody rubbish'. On another, a lady in Morrison's wanted not to talk about anything I had written, but to get an explanation of the workings of my hearing aids.

If you have any comments, good, bad or indifferent, I'd be happy to hear from you by e mail – howardels@gmail.com.   Thank you for supporting the Ryedale Book Festival by buying this book. I hope that you will enjoy it.

Howard Croft
Old Malton, Spring 2016

2011

New columnist from Old Malton

Following my crushing Malton Ward defeat at the hands of Councillors Andrews, Burr and Hopkinson in the District Council elections I bolted South to spend some quality time with my daughter where, away from pitying looks and faint praise, I might lick my wounds. And restore my brutalised ego; for despite my shy insistence before the vote that I would certainly lose, in my more psychotic moments of self-admiration I fancied myself a winner. An unlikely eventuality, as we now all know, faced as I was by these giants of the political scene who got sand in their boots during campaigns fought when I, politically speaking, was still in short trousers. I was no match for their wiles and knavish tricks.

Imagine, then, my dismay when, at an evening drinks party intended to distract me from my grief, I was confronted by an officer from another district council who, knowing of my electoral humiliation, felt the need to explain how local government works, to restore my self-esteem. What I had failed to win was not Power, a valuable commodity, but Office, a worthless bauble. Power is in the hands of Officers; Members merely hold office. I swear I could hear the initial capitals.

My failure to grasp this important truth, he said, had led me to exaggerate my loss, which was no loss at all. What, I asked him, would he be doing with all this power, under the new but toothless regime? Answer: To continue to pull the wool over the eyes of the Council Members, of course, and to devote himself to stopping people doing things. He was full of the success he and his colleagues had enjoyed in stamping out most of the Royal Wedding street parties. Saying No was clearly his mission and consulting his "stakeholders" an important device for creating obfuscation and delay in its service.

Though not himself a Planning Officer he took pride in that department's achievements in turning down planning applications. Covering as it does a large conservation area, rich with opportunities to disappoint, his co-workers not only score high marks here but are able also to create prosecution opportunities for Climate Change Officers charged with monitoring heat-loss from dwellings, by forbidding the installation of double glazing. He appeared to regard the wish to double glaze as roughly on a par with the wish to abduct a child.

What would he do that is positive? Answer: Anything we fancy that is legal and affordable. Beneficial and desirable too? Not a bit of it. Surely all four criteria would be applied in Ryedale, if, for example, should be a proposal (which as an opponent to the sale I would keenly support) to erect a statue of Councillor Andrews on Wentworth Street car park. I fear, however, that the sale would be necessary if the "affordability" test were to be passed to permit such a monument.

As fast as my skinny legs would go, I ran home where there is no army of power-crazed blotter jotters and pen pushers, but instead a phalanx of elected Members, who by their steely determination and mighty intellect will ensure that we are, as Cromwell said, properly governed. If only I were one of their number; grateful though I am to the voters who took a punt on a rank outsider, I wish there had been sixty more – then I would have been.

Take the shaker scandal with a big pinch of salt

It has been reported in national newspapers that a local council has bought salt shakers with unusually small holes, and sent officers round all the fish and chip shops in Grimsby, confiscating existing dispensers and substituting their own.

They have instructed the chippie staff to conceal the new shakers under the counter, producing them only if and when customers ask for them.

A bit like it's going to be with fags. It is not the first time a council has done this – I think it happened in Stockport – but in Grimsby? I bet they're quaking in their boots in Hull. And in Wetwang.

Why is this being done? It is part of the battle against high blood pressure.

This makes me worry about the kind of people employed in local government, who have so little insight into human behaviour.

I like my food salted just the way I like it; faced with a miserly shaker, I just shake a little longer until I get it right.

And why do chip shops favour shakers that deliver a generous serving with from a single wrist action? Because more genteel affairs would create a pinch point and customers would be backed up waiting to use them.

You have only to have been a customer to figure this out, but the people involved are so full of missionary zeal and a liking for enforcement that they can't think straight.

It is odd that local government has busied itself in recent years with health intervention. Obesity is another one. Almost every initiative coming out of town halls has tagged on the end the clincher – "and it will help combat obesity".

If the town halls had a fraction of the medical expertise they fancy themselves to possess they would realise that multi-factorial causes underlie obesity, and it is difficult to manage. Were it not so, there would be fewer plump doctors and nurses knocking about.

I noticed a fair number of porkers when I was hanging about in out-patients at York recently.

You may remember TV news footage last year of a school in lock-down to prevent the pupils visiting the chippie at lunchtime, in which crowds of furious mothers were filmed posting parcels of fish and chips through the railings to their children. They were not furious about a restricted diet, but at being bossed about by "officials".

How, I wonder, do town halls decide which medical conditions they will take on. Why obesity and hypertension, and not testicular cancer, say, or irritable bowel syndrome, or human papilloma virus? All afflictions that cause misery to many. Not romantic enough, I expect.

I was amused to read, a few days after the Grimsby chip shop scandal hit the headlines, a report from a group of clinical scientists claiming that a study of thousands of patients had shown that those with a high salt intake suffered fewer strokes and heart attacks than those with a low intake.

Will the busybodies acknowledge that they may have been killing their constituents, or client base as they would say, and nip out to return the shakers they had stolen and confiscate their own back?

I doubt it. After all, organisations that can appoint Climate Change Managers with a straight face are unlikely to shrink from practising a little medicine on the side – and, like Doctor, think they know best.

Let's hear it for blue

It has been reported in the clinical journal *The Laryngoscope* that medical researchers at the Charing Cross, Stoke Mandeville, andthe Royal Marsden hospitals have identified a link between the onset of deafness and taking impotence medication such as Viagra and Cialis.

The hearing loss may affect one or both ears, and it may be permanent. Medicines watchdogs across the world have been alerted.

The national press has picked this up – how could they resist – and the hundreds of thousands of men in Britain who wolf down these wonder drugs will be forming feverish queues at audiology clinics everywhere. They have my sympathy, of course.

But what about the rest of us, the "innocent" victims whose deafness has been caused by exposure to loud noise, ear infections and over-indulgence in transatlantic flights?

Are we, who until now have sported our digital aids without concern as we swagger about town on a Saturday morning, going to be suspected of doping ourselves to boost our mojo like dodgy athletes? Perhaps vilified in the streets by sniggering urchins or, worse, pestered by disappointed housewives – who can say?

Will the audiology clinics become places of embarrassment, even shame, so that gents such as myself stay away to the detriment our own auditory acuity? Will they, like the VD clinics of old, change their names to disguise their purpose, and arrange access through unmarked doors on side-streets behind the hospital?

There is an easy solution, with almost no cost implications.

Hearing aids for "the innocently deaf" should continue to be supplied in a choice of two colours – silver and pink – but those with self-inflicted hearing loss should be offered only blue, famously the colour of Viagra tablets. Thus there will be no doubt; if you spot a chap in Morrison's lurking about with what appear to be blue prawns tucked behind his ears, you'll know precisely what you are dealing with.

But what about the chaps with no prawns?

Might he not have popped them into his pocket for the duration of his shopping trip, and fooled us all? Compulsory hearing aids for all men over 35, perhaps, colour to be determined by their doctors.

On a personal note, if I may, let me say that during my entire childhood I was plagued by terrible otitis media that even the most powerful first generation antibiotics could not touch, relief coming only after years of waiting for the services of a decent ENT surgeon.

As an adult, in the course of my work, I flew close to a million miles, in the later stages crossing the Atlantic twice a month.

And my wife kicks up the most terrible racket in the kitchen banging pots and pans together, even when performing simple tasks like poaching an egg. Just in case you were wondering.

But it is not all bad news on the medical front. We are now told that drinking six or more cups of coffee a day protects you against at least six cancers, whereas last year we were confidently advised that more than three would cause your liver to explode.

So maybe the blue prawn tactic will be short-lived when "scientists" discover that deafness, far from being implicated in impotence in fact clears it up. What?

I'm deadly serious

When I retired I realised that the next significant life event would be less welcome than earlier ones had been, and more terminal– an encounter with the Grim Reaper. I considered my options for disposal. The green option, perhaps, with a reed basket and incineration? Burial at sea, maybe – is it allowed?

I finally decided to go the old fashioned route. A sturdy coffin, crafted from expensive English oak, perhaps with a mouse carved on it if the budget allows, certainly none of your MDF rubbish, and a quiet spot in a tidy graveyard. With this decided I legged it down to Old Malton cemetery to meet the sexton and pick out my plot – plots, actually, since we decided against the "stacking" method, cheaper though it is.

The town clerk let me have a couple at £210 a pop, which is good value – in York it's nearer £800.

I should add that prices are going up, which shows there is a futures market in final resting places, so if times get hard we could revert to the stacking idea, flog the spare and make a profit on the deal.

Get down there. As they say at Morrison's, when they're gone they're gone.

So there we are. Or will be. And you should see the location: in plain view is the *Royal Oak* public house, with the Wolds beyond.

I later told Marion and Duncan Hunter at the pub that I expect them, when the time comes, to give me a little wave from their garden, preferably weekly on a Thursday, which is pie night – my favourite.

As it happened, an hour or so after completing this business I hurried down to Morrison's to buy a bottle of Shiraz, for celebration purposes, where I ran into Marion at the checkout.

Still excited by my own cleverness, I gave a full account of my morning's work to her and the checkout lady who joined in, as they do. They were aghast. Their view was that it is unthinkable to make a purchase in anticipation of an eventuality one does not care to dwell on.

What sort of an attitude is that? If we were to be guided by that principle we would never buy toilet rolls or a plastic mac, and then where would Morrison's be?

So, I'm all set. A place for my descendents to visit in perpetuity (well, 99 years actually, after which the town clerk wants the plots back), bearing expensive blooms and, no doubt in my mind, deeply wailing. None of this off-hand "well, he had a good innings" stuff from them, or I'll want to know the reason why.

The next job is to plan the funeral, at St Mary's obviously, and the bash afterwards – pies at the *Oak* if we can get in.

And some Shiraz from Morrison's, but only if it's on offer.

Perchance to dream

Since I retired I have suffered from episodes of insomnia, a result, I suppose, of not working; I rarely exhaust myself now.

I nod off OK, but often wake in the early hours. At first I didn't worry too much about this.

I saw the time between waking at four and rising at seven to walk the dog as an opportunity to read cheap fiction. However, it did mean that by ten I was ready for lunch, and by three I was wanted a nap.

Not a bad life, you may think, but somehow it didn't seem right and I found that I was as prone to guilt as to insomnia.

I tried the usual remedies; cocoa didn't help, Horlicks sometimes did but was unreliable, and a few belts of Shiraz, although effective, produced unrefreshing sleep. Then I discovered Extra Strength Sleep Aid.

This is an over-the-counter sleep medication. I have always been dubious about pills available without a prescription, believing that doctors like to stay in control of the good stuff as a way of driving up demand for their services, but Sleep Aid is a cracker.

You know it's going to do the trick because of the warning on the box – "may cause drowsiness".

That and the fact that the chemist won't let you buy more than one packet, as I soon discovered. I suppose it didn't help that I confided to my plan to build up a stockpile under the mattress "just in case", but even my promises not to do anything silly wouldn't budge her.

A helpful chap waiting behind me, hearing all this, said, "Give us your money, mate. I'll get you another one".

And he did. As an old school friend, who chairs a magistrates' bench, complained, "I am trusted to decide on guilt and innocence, to impose fines and even to send people to prison, but I am not trusted with two packets of paracetamol".

If you try this product there is, apart from drowsiness, another side-effect to be on the look out for. It makes you dream.

Not those dreams that evaporate as soon as you wake up; these stay with you all day.

For several consecutive nights I was a professional tennis player competing at Wimbledon, which is odd since I have never played the game, or had much interest in it.

Anyway, I was doing rather well, thanks in part to a loyal band of fans who cheered me on, until I was knocked out in the semis by Rod Laver.

Fair enough, but I swear his last return was out. I was disappointed not to get to meet the Duchess of Kent and Cliff Richard.

I mentioned these dreams to a doctor friend who told me that he thought the Shiraz was the more likely culprit, and advised me to switch to Merlot. But I think I'll stay as I am.

I don't mind the dreams. Some of them are a bit unsettling, but there is always the chance I'll be picked to play for England against the Aussies.

A supermarket spat

So, the supermarket wars are hotting up nicely.

The news that Aldi have retired hurt surprised no-one – the empty car park at Lidl was easy to interpret – and indeed I have been predicting it for months.

What did surprise me was Sainsbury backing out of Wentworth Street. I thought that was a done deal.

Perhaps I spend too much time listening to the seductive voices of conspiracy theorists.

I have no experience in retail business so I really cannot comment on all this – not that it stops some people pronouncing with authority that I suspect is as bogus as it is unconvincing.

I hear low murmuring against Tesco now that Sainsbury is out of play, with sniffy suggestions that it is a comparatively *infra dignitatum* establishment.

I hope that we are not going to see an outbreak of the kind of snobbery so commonly found in towns in the south. "We absolutely *depend* on Tesco, my dear. It keeps the riff-raff out of Waitrose." You know the type.

Reading the feverish press reports about recent developments and forthcoming planning challenges, I thought that Janet Waggott was rather disingenuous when dealing with the Council's planning role.

She is correct in saying that it is common practice for councils to process and adjudicate on proposals they have themselves put forward, but she did not deal with the specific conflict of interest issue arising from two mutually exclusive proposals now on the table, one from the Council and another from the Fitzwilliam Estate.

They should recuse themselves, and their chums from the East Riding are too cosy a substitute.

And just because something is common practice doesn't make it right, even without a conflict of interest. In the Essex/Suffolk area, which has the highest concentration of listed buildings in the country, there is a small town whose high street is a conservation area where almost every building is listed, many of them Tudor.

There is a very fine old school building – I think Jacobean – set back from the road beyond lawns. It is one of the most striking buildings in the street.

Not that anyone is struck by it now because they have built on the lawn a red brick block that presents to the street its windowless rear and almost completely obscures the view of the old school.

What goes on inside I do not know, but it resembles nothing more that a detention centre for illegal immigrants.

Who owns the school? The council. Who granted permission? The same council.

Any application half as egregious from a homeowner of business would have received short shrift, and rightly so. I am sure that there are many examples of planning authorities granting themselves such exceptional leave to set their own interests above considerations of heritage.

Think of the Milton Rooms, and blush; aluminium framed, double glazed windows in a listed building!

Anyway, back to the supermarkets. I seldom shop in Tesco and Sainsbury's, in York or anywhere else, and when I do it is only to explore the offers on the wine shelves, which usually disappoint.

Asda on the other hand is a cracking spot for top notch booze bargains, but now we've got one coming to Malton I'll be able to stay away from York altogether. Unless I need some new spats, that is.

Can't compete with Curly

I am expecting a visit from my grandchildren, Archie and Imogen No-one teaches you how to be a grandfather, except by example your own, but there seems to be a general expectation that you should be interesting.

My difficulty is that my paternal grandfather I never knew – he died shortly after I was born – which leaves me with my mother's Dad.

How can I possibly match him? For a start, he was a gipsy, or as he used to say "A True Romany", whose encampment was by the gates of a large, gentleman's house in Tolpuddle, Dorset.

The gentleman in question employed a pretty maid, Jane.

An attachment was formed with grandfather, the pair of them ran away together and they didn't stop running until they reached Hull where they settled.

So far, so Mills & Boon – whirlwind romance, pretty young domestic, dashing gentleman of the road.

By the time I got to know him he (and Jane) had experienced eventful times that included a few years in the workhouse, losing a leg at Ypres (not Jane, obviously), and a few police cautions for "borrowing" horses to get home from the pub after one too many – taking and riding away, I suppose they called it.

He was a well-known and popular figure in the area of Hull where he lived, and my twin sister and I were also well-known; partly in my case because of my stunning physical beauty, but mainly because we were twins and we belonged to Curly, grandfather's nickname.

One day we were playing out in the terrace waiting for him to come home from work when he spotted us and took us off to the Penny Bun Shop to buy cream cakes.

Eventually we were missed, and there was a panic.

We had been seen by the only person in East Hull who did *not* know Curly who reported having seen us being led away by a disreputable old man.

Just as I was selecting a Devonshire split the police burst into the bun shop and pounced on gramps – but didn't hold him long, for they did know him, and us too, but marched us back to grandma who gave him a pasting I doubt he forgot.

I thought it was very exciting – a sort of Spaghetti House Siege without guns, and all too quickly over.

He used to leave two piles of pennies on the dresser for us which, after distribution he would recoup by rolling up his trouser leg and encourage us to post in the slot at the knee of his tin leg and hear them rattle down into the foot.

Once all the money had been returned to him in this way he would unstrap the leg and hop around the parlour for our entertainment – entertainment that we had to pay for. It delighted us, of course, and it was many years before I realised that not all grandfathers could perform this trick.

How can I compete with stuff like this? A trip on a steam train from Pickering is all very well but it won't be as memorable as the bun shop incident, not unless the police surround our carriage at Newtondale Halt and slap the cuffs on me.

Castle Howard is all very well in its way, but I'll be keeping both my legs on and where's the fun in that?

I'm afraid I shall be a grave disappointment in the grandparental stakes. I am working on ways to get the pocket money back but it will be dull by comparison.

That's weddings for you

My daughter Helen got married last week. I rarely accept invitations to weddings- I would rather sit on a spike than attend one – but in this case an exception had to be made.

The marriage itself took place in Bishop's Stortford, where the District Council is planning to sell off its car parks for over a hundred million to a supermarket developer. I managed to find time in my busy schedule to sign a petition in protest – twice.

The ceremony was remarkable in two ways: first because I had never before seen Helen sporting false eyelashes, and second because the ring bearer was her 18 month old Labrador, Rufus.

They both did very well, especially Rufus who managed to get through the whole thing without disgracing himself despite his gastro-intestinal system being in uproar. Helen wisely took him to the vet the day before to get him pharmaceutically "corked up" for the occasion.

Helen and Søren put on a self-catered reception for about sixty at their home in Quendon, of which you are unlikely to have heard.

It is located in Essex, the next village along from the village of Ugley, once celebrated for *The Ugley Women's Institute* until, a few years ago, when the ladies changed the name to *The Women's Institute (Ugley Branch)*, now widely ridiculed.

All this lies under the regime of Uttlesford District Council, which has no car parks to sell some time was saved there.

Some of the cooking was sub-contracted out to various members of the family, including myself. I contributed a vast cauldron of chilli con carne, my special thing, which looked especially tasty alongside some very ordinary lasagnes provided by ladies who looked surprisingly pleased with themselves when their offerings were brought to the table with, in my view, more flourish than was justified.

I was gratified to notice at the end, before the end in fact, that my effort had been wolfed down in its entirety while there was plenty of lasagne going begging. I didn't say anything.

What it is about weddings that makes otherwise sensible people loosen their grip on their sanity? For several weeks leading up to

"The Day" I was badgered by female relatives to buy new shoes – nothing else, just shoes.

My natty but not new linen suit from M&S was nodded through without comment, but new shoes had to be bought.

I gave in, despite owning several serviceable pairs, some recently purchased from *Goody Two Shoes* in Finkle Street at unbelievable prices, and bought a nifty brown boot for seventy quid, reduced from a price no sane man would pay.

They attracted many admiring glances, I noticed.

Søren, my son-in-law as I now must call him, is a Dane. It's all very well these days, but let us not lose sight of the fact that they crossed the North Sea with no good in mind.

At least they marry our daughters now, rather than taking the more robust approach of years gone by. There is one benefit of having a Dane in the family – if ever you fancy a bacon sandwich there's always someone happy to keep you company.

I had to make a speech. My older sister (by three hours – the most important three hours in her life) was quick to give advice. "Well, if you really feel you must say something, keep it short, keep to the point, don't embarrass yourself with what you think is your cleverness, and for goodness' sake smarten yourself up."

That's weddings for you, and it's why I steer clear if I can. And if I can't I always try to leave before the fighting starts.

Undercover detective work

I have been undercover, spending several mornings in the Fine Food Theatre disguised as a waitress, my good ear cocked for loose talk. This after all is where the political cognoscenti gather to "share"; my time was not wasted. I can report here for the first time that Ryedale District Council is negotiating the sale of Norton to the East Riding for a cool five million.

This is part of a wider scheme to improve the air quality at Butcher Corner, involving not only the dynamiting of County Bridge but also the erection a pedestrian-only toll booth on the Railway Street Bridge. "This is not primarily about money" an insider quipped as I brought him a bacon roll and helped him with his bib. Norton, like post-war Berlin, will find itself surrounded by a hostile District; residents wishing to go to Beverley to pay their council tax will be escorted in convoys of cars as far as Wetwang, under the protection of East Yorkshire police.

Sources are characteristically tight-lipped about what the five million will be spent on, but I can report that several Council officers have been spotted browsing in Malton Motors - they weren't looking at Minis – and the Chief Executive has been seen fingering expensive curtain fabrics in Boyes's. Hoping for a comment I tried to contact Colonel Hemesley, only to be told that he was unavailable, having for the past three days been locked in his garden shed, cleaning his duelling pistols. Still heavily disguised as a slip of a girl, I attempted to quiz a representative of the Fitzwilliam Estate only to be told, "Be off with you, you little minx. Fetch me a toasted teacake, and make it snappy!" Of Councillor Paul Andrews there has been no sign. Well placed sources tell me that a writ of habeas corpus has been drawn up, and there are fears for his safety. But on whom will it be served?

Of course, Beemers all round for council executives and smart new curtains in the executive suite at Ryedale House won't make much of a hole in the five big ones, so what's going on? A clue, perhaps, is in the unusual appearance of surveyors and estate agents furtively poking about in St Mary's, Old Malton Churchyard, making notes on clipboards. Residents whose home backs onto the churchyard are speculating that the ideal site has been identified for a new, larger Ryedale House, and that RDC is preparing to give itself permission to demolish the priory church. One resident, who does not wish to be named, commented that the church, which does not have mains services, is in dilapidated state due to its great age and could easily transfer its functions to modern Portakabins located in a field by Eden Camp. She added that the site of the old Ryedale House would be the perfect spot for a Harvey Nicks, filling a scandalous gap in Malton's retail offering. I shall keep you informed.

So, what was it like going undercover dressed up as a waitress? The disguise wasn't perfect (the moustache was a bit of a giveaway) but it fooled most people, and those it didn't fool were too shy to comment. I can tell you the tips were poor, but I did attract some lavish compliments and a number of interesting propositions. One local worthy invited me to go with him to the races, with an overnight stay in York, and another, claiming to have a penthouse there, suggested a weekend in Bridlington. I resisted their blandishments – these married men! The offer of a week in a caravan in Skegness, all found, was more of a temptation, but Lincolnshire?

Excitement over old bones

Great excitement in Old Malton last week. After a routine day in which I passed my annual blood pressure test *summa cum lauda*, as my old Latin master used to say, and hopped on and off the scales without raising nurse's eyebrow (the advantage of this obesity plague is that stout is the new skinny), the evening brought more drama and excitement than I have had since the old king died in the fifties. Human remains had been found only a few yards from the garden seat on which Mrs Croft and I enjoy a glass or two of the white of a summer evening before retiring indoors for some red.

The discovery was made next door by the outbuildings of the old vicarage, which is being renovated in readiness for new residents. This is what happened. We had spent a bit of time in the Royal Oak and as we made our way home, a little unsteadily in Mrs Croft's case, who put this down to some prawns she had eaten the week before, I noticed unusual police activity next door. We hurried past, anxious to catch the start of *The Great British Bake-off*, and I forgot all about it until ten o'clock when the door bell rang and I was confronted by two police officers. One of them was a female, which was a bit worrying– if I have read my Inspector Morse books correctly this betokens bad news. I was not to worry, I was told, but I should know that human remains had been found, that my neighbour's house had been cordoned off and it would be guarded overnight by a constable in a police car parked by my back gate. My first thought was that I had been living next door to a Fred West character but luckily, before I sent them off to Castle Howard Road to feel the collar of the previous resident, I remembered that this was Reverend John Manchester, an unlikely suspect in a brutal murder.

The fact that my house and John's former home were built, centuries ago, on part of what is still St Mary's churchyard was an early clue, spotted instantly by the police. And by me; sadly, my hopes of charging rubber-neckers a fiver each to come into my garden and peer over the wall faded fast. And so it was that in less than twenty-four hours the "expert from London" had been and declared life extinct and the bones old, and the constables withdrew to concentrate on more thrilling duties that sitting through night in a dark churchyard, fighting sleep.

I was spoken to by a number of police officers all of whom were very reassuring, telling me that I had no cause for concern, which seemed a bit odd – if the idea of human remains nearby worried me, why would I have bought a house over looking a graveyard, a house, what is more, that has a couple of documented graves in the garden.

During the time I have been contributing this column to the *Mercury* a number of people have stopped me in the street or come up to me in shops to tell me how much they enjoy it; Mrs Croft refers to them, rather acidly, as "your fan club", and accuses me of having developed a swagger as I make my way along Saville Street to my hairdressers. It's very good to hear such remarks, of course, but a conversation in the *Wentworth Arms* dimmed the rosy glow. It went like this:

First Old Codger: Are you that fella that writes that column in the Mercury?
Second Old Codger (puffing himself up): Yes, I am. What do you think of it?
First Old Codger: I think nowt to it. It's rubbish!

Collapse of stout party.

A castle wouldn't suit

In the late fifties my father bought his first car – a 1936 Singer Bantam, a small two-door saloon with a lethal looking mascot of a cock bantam in flight mounted on the front of the bonnet. Pedestrians lucky enough to survive any impact would have been fatally speared by the rooster. He paid twenty pounds for it and sold it several years later for fifteen.

The first decent run out in it was from Hull to Castle Howard, which my parents very much liked to visit, which they had often done in the thirties on a Brough Superior motorcycle.

I doubt if the house was open to the public – they would just have looked at it from the road. Dad's main purpose setting out in the Singer was to see how she would cope with Staxton hill. Dad, being a lorry driver, knew the value of a tight load so off we went, two up in the front and three kids in the back. Staxton Hill was not a problem.

My mother named me after the Castle Howard, which is why I have always taken almost proprietorial interest in it; when it starred in *Brideshead Revisited* I could hardly hold my water I was so proud.

Father disapproved of the name on the grounds that felt it suited only to men who are "not as other men", a phrase I didn't understand until adulthood but which made me vaguely uneasy as a child, an unease that lingers still.

So, it was with some pleasure and much pride when I read that my house had been identified as a top world tourist destination. The architecture and history of the house were summarised in the press reports and cited as reasons for its popularity, which I suppose is true but I think it goes deeper than that, or shallower depending on your point of view.

Mrs Croft and I are season ticket holders, going there frequently and invariably taking any house guests along, smugly announcing "look what we've got just down the road".

They are always impressed. There are two reasons, I think.

Firstly, it is astonishingly well run. The staff are without exception friendly and helpful.

It would be invidious to single anyone out but I'm going to do it anyway – Mr & Mrs Foxton are outstanding. Always a warm welcome at the plant centre where Mr Foxton dispenses advice with the reassuring air of an Old Testament sage, and Mrs Foxton applies a discount if you are a season ticket holder and offers small treats to our flat coated retriever, a regular visitor since she was a puppy.

The signage is excellent, always the indication of well run outfit, designed to assist rather than, as is so often the case elsewhere, to prohibit.

Not a "Keep off!" sign in sight, and the word "please" everywhere to be seen. The assumption seems to be that visitors are likely to know how to behave.

Secondly, there is something there for us all. The house, of course, and the grounds, the Plant Centre, the Courtyard shops, the children's play area, and the Courtyard Restaurant where they once served excellent full English breakfasts on Sunday mornings, but sadly no longer do. We frequently took our visitors there to fill them with bacon and eggs before pointing them in the direction of the A1.

However, grand though the house is I couldn't live in it. The last thing the Howards want is someone like me feeling sorry for them, but sometimes I do. It's just too big.

My day always begins with the search for my spectacles, not much of a chore where I hang my hat, but it annoys the hell out of Mrs Croft so Castle Howard wouldn't suit us. Anyway, well done, Castle Howard – more grease to your elbow.

Bad reputation at stake

Recently, I was chatting to one of the local political nabobs, known for his stern criticism of Ryedale District Council, when he surprised me by saying that, while not perfect, RDC is pretty good, especially when compared with so many similar bodies.

I think that he is right, though it is not a view lightly to be expressed, especially to single issue fanatics, at a time when the Council is taking so much flack about the Wentworth Street car park.

This is partly its own fault; people on both sides of this question seem to agree that the Council's public relations ineptitude has unnecessarily inflamed matters and earned it few friends.

What local councils everywhere have, though they seem not to see it, is a reputation management problem, created for them all by the actions of the worst of them.

Examples: a council whose litter warden spotted an unemployed man leaving a post office where he had cashed his benefit Giro and carelessly dropped a tenner on the pavement, supported the warden's decision to issue an £80 penalty for littering.

Another, where an officer who sent an aggressive, threatening letter to a partially sighted resident in his nineties for placing an item in the wrong recycling box, repudiated criticism in the local press saying, "The rules apply equally to all".

Well, in a civilised society they don't; the weak, the infirm and the confused get special consideration.

He was supported by his employer. One wonders where councils find these people, whose crass inflexibility and fondness for bullying taint local government everywhere.

These are just a couple of examples of official high handedness taken from the many that appear in the national press almost weekly.

They enter the public consciousness as "the kind of things that councils do".

Three things, I believe, have created a climate of suspicion and mistrust in which are ready to assume the worst.

Firstly, in her enthusiasm to break the power of unions Margaret Thatcher abolished central wage bargaining and passed it down to the local level – she put the Gloucester Old Spots in charge of the trough, with results that are now only too evident.

Secondly, under the RIPA legislation, designed to deal with terrorism and serious crime, council officers were, unwisely, given considerable powers, which, they deployed with infantile gusto.

Even relatively junior officers are said to be able to mount covert surveillance operations against residents more easily than police officers can do against criminals.

Finally, and most recently, it has emerged that some councils hand out credit cards to their staff without putting in place effective approval procedures.

Shockingly, one council revealed that items below £5000 were regarded as "below the radar" and so not scrutinised.

During my time in business I signed, or did not, a couple of thousand claims for expenses, many of them incurred on company cards.

Nothing was below the radar, and explanations ("who was at this dinner and why?") were frequently demanded. Local tax payers are used to encountering and tolerating low level incompetence in their dealings with the council, but corruption is quite a different matter as they quickly found out in Cornwall, the worst offender.

Practices have been reported in the press which, if accurately reported, would have led to criminal prosecution in my time. The worst have smeared even the best.

I said at the beginning that I take the view that RDC is a good deed in a naughty world, but I don't want you to run away with the idea that I see no ships.

I once used a council service for which there was a charge.

Just when I was wondering where the invoice had got to, I got a legal letter offering the possibility of prosecution.

The next time I used the service and after a month no invoice arrived, I legged it Ryedale House to sort it out, fearful for my reputation.

It took three visits over several weeks to get my money accepted.

Hilariously, a couple of autumns ago I was sweeping leaves outside my house when a bumptious fellow, claiming to be a council officer, jumped out of his car and demanded to know what I was doing.

Sweeping leaves, I confessed. You should not do that, he said, there are training and health and safety issues.

When I asked for his name, he jumped back into his car and roared off.

So, if you think there is anything a jobsworth can teach you about sweeping up, you know where to go.

Child maketh the man

By today's standards my childhood would be described as deprived – no telly, no central heating, outside privy, no books in the home, and not much money.

Dad was a lorry driver, not a well-paid occupation in the fifties. Before you go to your sleeve for a lace hankie and stifle a sob, or, if you are social worker, reach for a court order and take me into care (I am, after all, an orphan now, and willing to consider adoption if the right couple can be found), let me tell you that it was a happy childhood, with many happy memories.

I suppose, even though I thought nothing of the "deprivations" at the time, they have left their marks.

Take the outside privy. Unwillingness to step out into the yard in the dark to answer calls of nature allowed me to develop great fortitude in the bladder control department, the benefits of which I continue to enjoy.

During my final years of working I used to fly on a fortnightly schedule between London and Philadelphia. I had a deep reluctance to use the lavatories on 'planes, partly repelled by the over-abundance of other users but mainly because they have no windows.

I cannot explain this. Perhaps, deep down, I believe that if I can't see out the 'plane is more likely to crash. And so it was that I was able to leave my flat in London, going before I went, Tube it to Heathrow, take the 'plane to Philly where I would take a short cab ride home, and only then attend to a call of nature, twelve hours later.

Whenever a doctor suggests a prostate specific antigen (PSA) test I describe this routine and he quickly turns his attention to something else – usually my alcohol intake. The "not much money" feature has left a less positive legacy; I fret several times a day, mostly in the night, about not having any.

As a result I am a rather frugal person, more inclined to squirrel money away than to spend it. Mrs Croft, on the other hand, I can only describe as a bit of a spender.

I watch in horror (and in silence) as she hoses the stuff about, mostly on non-essentials, new frocks and the like. I reassure myself that we balance each other out, but this may be a self-deluding tactic.

I do wonder about it. Why, for example, when we are buying the ingredients for chilli con carne, my only truly virtuoso culinary performance, does she insist on getting two green peppers when my recipe calls for only one? I could, I suppose, put both in but that would distort the delicate balance of flavours that I have perfected over many years. I fancy there's a mystery in it.

But back to childhood. It's and odd fact, looking back, that as a small boy I was an enthusiastic reader of the Jennings books, tales of a group of boys in a boarding preparatory school, and I keenly looked forward every week to episodes of *The Barlows of Beddington*, also set in a boarding school, on the BBC Home Service.

I was fascinated by this alien world of matrons, tuck shops and postal orders from home, but I didn't envy it or want to be in it, any more than, when I read *Black Beauty*, I wanted be a horse and live in a stable.

Nor, when I won a scholarship to the grammar school on the posh side of town where I mixed with middle class boys whose lives were very different, the start of a process that led to me living in a house with several toilets (all indoors), did it bother me.

What does all this tell us? It tells us that Wordsworth spoke true when he wrote:

So was it when my life began;
So is it now I am a man.
The child is father of the man.

In other, less poetic words, I may worry about money more than is good for me - but my prostate's in cracking shape.

Hopes not resolutions

I thought that this might be an appropriate moment to review with you the highlights of my personal life during 2011, and to cast a sceptical eye at the next twelve months.

You will remember that 2011 was the year in which I staged my surprise bid to enter public life by running for office in the District Council elections. It was a bold move that rattled the local political establishment, but one in which, being made just as the potential for personal enrichment through dodgy expenses claims was savagely under attack, I revealed, according to my friends, characteristically poor sense of timing.

The electorate, with equally characteristic sound judgement, gave me the bum's rush, so it was academic in the end. But not without its lessons.

My chief supporter and mentor, my tactician if you like, was in favour of the sale of Wentworth Street car park. The fact that he and I disagreed, as we still do, on this great matter in no way inhibited our collaboration, but it did confuse some of my opponents who, with their finely attuned noses for such things, scented a duplicitous ploy and proceeded to portray me as a Janus-faced Hydra who represented a grave threat to the body politic. This revealed their deeply political nature, and also their failure to understand the nature of friendship. It would be invidious to mention names. You know who you are.

This chicanery may have cost me a few votes, but not so many as I suspect I gained from another attempt to discredit my candidacy by suggesting, not that I was concealing my real beliefs on key issues, but that I was concealing my true identity.

This was a clever move, disguised as an April Fool prank, orchestrated by certain members of staff (Dawn) at the Linton pet shop in the Market Place. Doctored copies of my election poster appeared in their window revealing me to be Alf Garnett, a character off the telly of strong but unwholesome opinions. The reaction on the doorsteps was immediate – I had instantly become popular, treated like an old disreputable uncle, but a sound thinker nevertheless.

After a couple of days, they took the posters down, much to my dismay. Had it not been a serious criminal offence I would have offered them a brown envelope full of the folding stuff to reinstate them.

It is my firm belief that, if those counterfeit posters had remained in place for the duration of the campaign, I would have been swept to victory on a landslide the like of which has never before seen in Ryedale.

Beside this attempt to insert myself into weighty affairs of state, more personal landmarks may seem trivial but I shall record them anyway. My son presented me with another grandchild, Imogen, who is now an eight-month old delight.

Even more of a delight is to watch her bewitching and manipulating her father much as his sister used to manage me. Used to? Who am I kidding – it never stops, they can't help it.

Speaking of my daughter, she got married during the year – I may have mentioned this. Against the better judgement of some family members I made a speech, described by one witness to it as "unusual". I took this as a compliment, though I doubt that it was so intended.

So, what of 2012? I'm not one for resolutions – if, as in the past I have, I resolve to give up alcohol for a month I tend to spoil it after a week by rewarding myself by cracking open a bottle of red for managing seven days, and away we go.

But hopes I do have. I hope that in the interests of doing something about my thickening waist I shall manage to improve my behaviour around pies – the talk is of little else in the *Royal Oak*. I hope also that Mrs Croft will refrain from commenting, when I grumble about my stiff knees in the morning, "Don't worry about it; you don't look a day over 70". She means well (I think), but 70 is still some way off. And I hope that my prostate will make it through another year.

It's not much of a wish list, I know that, but it's all I have to offer. So, Mrs Croft joins me in wishing you all a happy and healthy New Year.

2012

A lunch full of decibels

I still call it the Christmas break, but being retired it is hardly that for me; I now spend *all* my time either reading cheap fiction and eating Jammy Dodgers, or lying down in a darkened room recovering from the night before.

Anyway, during the Christmas break Mrs Croft and I nipped down to Chichester in the gas-guzzler to pay our respects to the Mother-in-Law, who kindly took us out for lunch at a new restaurant there. It's a Raymond Blanc joint called *Brasserie Blanc* – I bet Raymond's marketing people were up all night coming up with that one.

The food was excellent, the acoustics terrible, made worse by the presence of a table full of what I took to be bank employees noisily celebrating their bonuses. The thing I don't like about French restaurants is their dogged refusal to serve any wine other than French, which I try to avoid.

In my experience it ranges from "just about drinkable" down to "absolute filth" and is, like the French themselves I suppose, unreliable and unpredictable. I was first warned off it by the great re-labelling scam years ago when thousands of cases of *vin tres ordinaire* were re-packaged as chateau bottled high end stuff and priced up accordingly.

Then came the sorbitol scandal. French vineyards were adding sorbitol, a sweetening agent, to their reds to make them more palatable, more like the products of New World wine makers who were stealing market from the French. This fraudulent practice was banned by the EU and all existing stocks had to be destroyed.

It just so happened that New World reds contained high levels of sorbitol naturally, hence their appeal, not the result of adulteration.

All these stocks held in the EU (mainly the UK of course) also had to be ditched, and not only that, they, mainly South American suppliers, had to go to the trouble and expense of artificially extracting naturally occurring sorbitol to the levels found in the vinegary, undoctored French varieties.

The advantage went to the French. Or so they thought. They reckoned without me – I upped my consumption to punish them.

What with the nightmare acoustics and the raucous bankers, faces purple with greed, it was in many ways a trying episode and I found my attention wandering. I noticed two couples at the table opposite who seemed to be having a good time, one of them wiring in to a cauldron of mussels with obvious relish.

Although I couldn't hear their conversation – I couldn't hear it at my own table – I detected what I thought were the cadences of North Yorkshire speech, and in fact I thought I recognised the chap sucking on the mussels, though as is turned out I was wrong about the latter.

It was an itch I had to scratch and as we got up to go I spoke to the sea food enthusiast and asked him where he was from. Londonderry, he told me, in an unmistakeable Yorkshire accent, but he was no Ulsterman.

It turns out – you probably know this – that there is a village near Northallerton that goes by that name. I had a very pleasant chat with him, fellow by the name of Ron Exelby, owner of the Leeming Bar service station on the A1 which I know well, during which we consoled each other for being so far from home.

It was the highlight of my day was that. For him I think it was the mussels.

Reflecting upon the fact that we had just the one bottle of wine with our meal, not a common occurrence in my experience, I was reminded of something I read recently.

Someone, I forget who, said that the most beautiful words in the English language are "Do you think we can manage another bottle?" – especially when spoken at lunchtime. I'll have them inscribed on my gravestone if the Council will allow it.

However, the biggest surprise of my Christmas was when my clever economist friend, Michael Taylor, appeared at my door with a gift-wrapped chainsaw. Michael, a close student of this column, had noted my bitter complaint in December that, in spite of it appearing on my Christmas wish list every year, Santa had never obliged with one.

It is my suspicion that Santa is unduly influenced by Mrs Croft. I suspect also that Mrs Taylor, who didn't approve of his purchase of this essential piece of equipment when he made it, put the idea into his head to give it to me. Mrs Croft is fuming.

Anyway, such is the power of the press that I now have my own chainsaw. I now wish that I had expressed a longing for a Faberge egg. Next year perhaps.

How about Honours for no-hopers?

What with the 'phone hacking and corruption investigations, the Hillsborough affair, the West Coast Mainline fiasco, and the emerging Jimmy Savile business, possibly implicating the BBC and other public bodies, the number of prominent people on remand, already large, seems likely to grow.

Senior media figures, high end police officers, civil servants and politicians are well represented in all this, and it is among such people Honours are most commonly to be found. There is already talk of rescinding Jimmy Savile's knighthood, although Whitehall mandarins are suggesting that Honours cannot be reclaimed post mortem; the only reason why seems to be that mandarins are saying it is so, which makes you wonder.

But it would, I suppose, be awkward if someone came up with a convincing case that Lord Nelson was a shoplifter, and HMQ asked for his peerage back.

As it is likely that there will soon be a significant harvest of confiscated CBEs and so on, some thought should be given to their redistribution. It is said that they are rationed (except for Whitehall civil servants, who get them automatically as they climb the slippery pole, irrespective of numbers and of merit), in which case they should be made available again.

But it would not be simple, as is the case with Olympic medals say; if the gold winner were discovered to have been a doper on the day, everyone would shuffle up a notch. If a knighted businessman were to be discovered to have had his hand trapped in the till, it would not be enough to go looking for another businessman both of whose hands had been constantly in plain view. It is possible, after all, that there might be more than one – then what would you do?

My idea is that they should be made available for the purpose of charitable fundraising. It would be quite a boost if an OBE were to feature as a prize in our Church's Christmas Fayre raffle, or a knighthood were to be offered at an auction of promises at the Rugby Club. In this way people who are otherwise seen to be no-hopers in the honours stakes, yet have the price of a raffle ticket, would be in with a chance and money would be raised for good causes.

This might also go some way towards correcting the current bias against those in more humble situations. I know a man, who knows his way around the system, who has nominated a number of worthy potential recipients for the MBE.

To make the case it is necessary to demonstrate significant achievements beyond occupational ones. Take a case: a midwife who has toiled for three decades ensuring safe and happy outcomes, has hadrecord numbers of babies named after her, and for whom Royal Mail has each to lay on a special van to deliver the Christmas cards sent by happy, grateful mothers.

In addition to this, she is always washing her hands, has successfully brought up a family, wormed the cat regularly, decorated the
spare room every three years and never smoked weed. She would
be a hard sell to the Honours Committee. On the other hand, take a
successful rock star, fabulously rich and "known to the police": up
pops a knighthood for "services to music". But services to midwifery
is not enough. I want a world in which there is a possibility, however
remote, of a dinner lady becoming a dame.

Thought should also be given to the possibility of children
inheriting their parents' honours, in the manner of the better type of
peerages. In this way we could celebrate historic family achievement.

Still, I wouldn't want to push things too far on the confiscation
front. It wouldn't do at all if I had to send my O Levels back if I were
caught cheating in a pub quiz. Not that I would.

It's the way you whistle

When I was training my flatcoated retriever, Rosie, I found
that, apart from morsels of food, the most valuable aid was a
whistle.

Not one of those ultrasonic jobs that dogs can hear but we can't;
I tried one of those, but I couldn't figure out whether the whistle
wasn't working or the dog wasn't.

Now, I don't need the edible treats – three short blasts on the
whistle is all, and in she comes.

When Morrison's extended their Malton store a year or so ago,
Mrs Croft's tiresome habit of wandering off became even more
problematic, so I thought, why not apply the same principle?

I decided to give it a try without telling her. To avoid the possibility
of being observed to fail by people who know me I first gave it a try in
Waitrose.

Off we went, me with a concealed whistle and a pocket full of Dolly
Mixtures, all ready for a trial run.

Sure enough, as soon as I paused to inspect the wine section, off
she went in search of I don't know what, detergent probably – her
favourite thing.

I gave three blasts and she instantly appeared, looking all eager – I
didn't even have to part with a Dolly Mixture.

What is more, my daughter, who I had forgotten was with us, also
appeared, from a different direction.

I get this sometimes on the morning walk along the Derwent; I
whistle up Rosie and before I know it I'm surrounded by Labradors

looking for a snack.

Since the successful experiment in Waitrose, which attracted quite a few disapproving looks from other shoppers (and admiring glances from their husbands) I have been using this technique on a regular basis in Morrison's without attracting any dark looks.

One of the assistants, Molly, saw me in action the other day and, looking me in the eye, said "I can't believe you did that". It's nice to get such recognition, and that's the difference between Morrison's and Waitrose; they welcome any contribution to the efficient running of the business.

I have a couple of concerns. One is that others will start to imitate me, and then where will we be? Whistles will be going off all over the place and I'll be surrounded by other people's wives, some of them expecting Dolly Mixtures.

The other is that Mrs Croft will one day appear at my side with a pheasant in her mouth, and we'll have to buy it.

A friend of mine with whom I shared my reunification technique has, in my view unwisely, started to extend it in other ways.

Now, when he claps his hands at bedtime, his wife immediately goes out into the garden which, apart from confusing his spaniel, could lead to some embarrassment.

Imagine, for example, being at a wedding reception in a smart hotel and, when the father of the bride claps his hands to get the speeches started, your wife nips out through the French windows. That wouldn't do at all.

My advice is to keep it simple, otherwise there'll be confusion. And don't try it at all if you don't like eating pheasant.

Elvis has left the building

We went to a bit of a do at Ken and Sylvia's last week, which is always a pleasure; their home, once a school, is one of the most interesting in Old Malton I think. Ours was also once a school, but there is no longer any obvious evidence of its past, which means that I can get rather boring about it, rather like those National Trust guides who get too wrapped up in their work.

Anyway, it was at this do that I took some heavy fire on account of my attitude to French wine, expressed recently on this page. Derek Fox, purveyor of game, was, appropriately enough, first up with both barrels in defence of St Emilion wine, as he was bound to do, being a grand Poo-Bah in the Jurade de St Emilion.

He knows a lot about wine, whereas I am merely an enthusiastic consumer, and he soon had me shivering in one of those conversational fox holes reserved for the uninformed but opinionated when confronted by an expert.

He took exception to my remarks about the former French practice of adulterating their reds with sorbitol. I thought, but was too shy to say, that recent revelations about the French practice of employing industrial grade gels, designed for use in cheap mattresses, in surgical prostheses might tend to lend credibility to my version of the sorbitol scandal. Best say nothing and look contrite.

Another guest, of an ethical bent, questioned whether I was thinking sufficiently carefully when writing about important matters, suggesting that I might inadvertently lead astray the unwary.

I hadn't really thought about this, but I have done so since and I have come to the conclusion that those who take anything I say as a reliable guide when ordering their lives must be very unwary indeed.

In any case, to take seriously my views on wine could lead at worst to a tendency to avoid French products, hardly a catastrophic outcome. However, I gave solemn undertakings as to my future conduct.

We decided to leave the party rather earlier than is usual for us, the reason for this being that I was feeling rather tipsy, but I didn't feel I could say this lest I be suspected of over-indulging our hosts' hospitality.

Largeing it, my son would say. The perfect alternative explanation came to me in a flash: we had to get home, I said, because Mrs Croft was anxious to watch some videos of *Blankety Blank*, kept by her since the eighties, her favourite show.

Which reminds me of a secretary I had years ago, who made a point of telling me every Tuesday that she had to leave promptly at five so as to sure not to miss *Blankety Blank*. Her keenness was based on her hope that one day Elvis would be a celebrity contestant. This was long after Elvis's death, and any suggestion by me that he had been called to higher service would make her tearful and even less inclined to stay on after five. The nearest I came to modifying her expectation that he would appear on the telly was by pointing out to her that he had been spotted in Colchester, working as a shelf-stacker in Tesco, living a quiet life away from the bright lights, and so unlikely to visit a television studio.

This sighting, reported in a tabloid newspaper, was made credible, it was said, by the fact that he was wearing his trade mark stage outfit, and it was widely believed by Elvis fans of the deluded variety. It seems strange to me that even the most credulous could accept that Elvis, fleeing celebrity, would go to earth in Colchester but continue to wear his fancy costume, and take a job in Tesco. If it was Waitrose I could understand it.

The point of all this, I suppose, is that if you are attracted to anything I say and tempted to act on it, first seek professional help.

When Rufus came to stay

As you may know, I have a dog, Rosie, a flat coated retriever, and my most affectionate and loyal friend; soon to be my only friend, my son says, if I don't make more of an effort to be less grumpy. Irascible may have been the word he used - he attended top-hole comprehensive. You may even have spotted me loping along the banks of the Derwent with her of a morning. Flat coats are an attractive breed, obedient and intelligent, but with a tendency to go self-employed at times, which keeps us on our toes. There was a large convention of these dogs and their owners at Castle Howard recently to which we were not invited; the familiar "no riff raff" situation. It was fully reported in *Country Life* magazine, which is not my publication of choice. I'm more of an *Acta Scandinavica Theologica* man myself. That and *Viz*.

Anyway, last week we had a canine guest. He, Rufus, is my daughter's Labrador, left in our care while she went to Florence on her honeymoon, squeezed in between her marriage last August and the birth of her first child this August. She runs a tight diary. Rufus, not what you would call a super-intelligent animal, as his slightly wall-eyed appearance suggests, is not so organised. Throughout the first day he watched, like stout Cortez on first looking into Chapman's Homer, as Rosie dutifully went through her routines, having on his face that expression of bewildered concentration that only the truly stupid can manage.

He is nevertheless an affectionate dog who likes nothing better than to truffle in his grandpa's moustache in search of edible debris, and he has great charm. Rosie was of course a bit put out by this boisterous intruder inserting himself between her and her master, and he, by Day Two, became depressed when he realised he had been abandoned by the feckless honeymooners. We were worried enough to move the knife block to a higher shelf in the kitchen. So, what with reassuring Rosie and consoling Rufus, we had quickly to transform ourselves into something resembling a Social Services Department but without the option of initiating care proceedings with a view to adoption.

Owning a dog is a responsibility, but caring for someone else's is a worry. They come with detailed instructions about dietary

preferences, medical routines – in Rufus's case twice weekly
ear hygiene of the most disgusting sort – which are a struggle to
understand, remember and implement (especially the ear business).
And health and safety is an issue. When my daughter saw the
Derwent before she swanned off to Leeds-Bradford, swollen and fast
moving as it was (the river, not the airport), she extracted from me a
solemn promise not to send Rufus in. First walk out, no sooner had
we entered the Gannock than both dogs hurled themselves into the
river like reckless schoolboys at Filey and had a fine time of it. This is
just between ourselves, mind.

As we're on the subject of dogs, and miscarriages of justice as
it happens, let me confide events surrounding a friend of mine,
a distinguished senior military officer. No names, no pack drill.
When he was out with them one of his two Springers, not normally
flighty animals, somehow got away from him later to be picked up
in the traffic by an NYP dog handler who was passing in his van. He
took the stray into protective custody and delivered it to its owner.
Usually, I would have thought, an immediate ASBO would have been
the order of the day and so it was: but it was slapped on the dog!
Could it be that the delinquent owner, who is known to the police,
escaped the personal ASBO because of his connections to Ryedale
House? For the avoidance of doubt or suspicion I should add that the
delinquent dog owner is not a member of my Wednesday Breakfast
Club, some of whom might fit the description. We wouldn't have him,
not even on the end of a barge pole.

Anyway, Rufus has gone home. 2012 will be known as "the year
Rufus came to stay". I miss him, hooligan though he is. I wonder
how he will cope with having a baby girl in the house come August.
I also wonder what she will be called, but prospective Mum and Dad
are being tight-lipped. Howardina is not a name you come across
everyday and it has quite a ring to it, as I am sure you will agree.

A Brazilian bottom-lift, sir?

A friend of mine was having his legs waxed recently when, out
of the blue, his therapist or beautician, waxer anyway, said
"Had you ever thought of having a Brazilian bottom-lift?" This is an
example of mission-creep, increasingly common these days, and very
irritating it is. What business is it of a leg waxer what's going on
elsewhere? We don't expect the doctor to look up from his
sigmoidoscope and murmur, "Don't you think it's about time you
changed your car?" Or the butcher to comment on the state of your

overcoat while he's butterflying your leg of lamb.

But everyone seems to be obsessed with surgical correction of physical imperfections; there is almost nothing else on Radio Four these days. Astonishingly, the demand for these procedures increases apace, exponentially one might say if one knew what it meant, in the main from women but men are fast catching up. Millions, literally, every year submit to the surgeon's lancet in futile attempts to stave off the effects of ageing and so, they believe, remain attractive. It simply doesn't work. It is true that pretty young women, what my father used to call popsies, no longer cast hot looks in my direction as I persuade myself they once did, but this is not because I am bald it is because I am on the dark side of sixty. Hair implants will do nothing about this; all it will do is leave me looking like a Chinese gooseberry, also on the dark side of sixty, and what good is that?

This morning (on Radio Four) a woman complained that she had been saddled with a £6000 debt following a face lift that had left her looking, in her words, "nothing like I had looked before". I thought that was the whole point. And on the telly a (good-looking) young woman described how she had undergone cosmetic breast augmentation surgery with which she was dissatisfied, and how she had submitted to a second procedure which she also found not to be up to snuff. After waiting for the second operation to heal she had booked herself in for a third attempt. She spoke as if she had been visiting her dressmaker. Astonishingly, she was presented as a role model in the matter of routine surgical refurbishment.

But back to the Brazilian bottom-lift. I have a rough idea of what this is, I think, but why is it "Brazilian"? I had thought that it was because you have to go to Brazil for one, but I am assured they are available in London, even in Leeds though I doubt if there is much demand there. The mystery remains. What seems to clear is that the demand for this enhancement is chiefly among men. What is the point? I am assured by those with long memories that in my youth my bottom was pert and widely admired; the talk was of little else at the Locarno Ballroom in Hull during the sixties. They assure me with equal confidence and kindness that this is no longer the case; unsur-prisingly after decades earning my living, for the most part, sitting down. Should I have the op? I doubt if I would emerge from the anaesthetic looking like a (Brazilian?) lounge lizard, or indeed an Italian sea captain all of whom seem to be very handsome. After all, the bald head, the protruding belly and the dowager hump would all remain. I'm afraid I would look like a badly made pot.

I'm not against a bit of titivation; we all trim our nails, spend money at the hairdressers and so on, but I draw the line at going under the knife. I know surgeons recommend it, but they would, it's their invariable solution when approached with a problem; to a man with a hammer, everything looks like a nail.

It's a dogger's life

Many notable people and events have come out the East Riding to make its natives proud, and as a native myself I share their pride. I shall mention only a few: the Bridlington Agreement, William Wilberforce, Tom Courtney, Maureen Lipman, "Lord" Prescott, and, that other comedian, Brian Rix. And David Whitfield, of course – remember him? But none of this prepared us for recent news from the county, courtesy of the *Daily Telegraph*: one of the nation's foremost dogging venues lies within its borders.

It appears that the hot spot centres on three lay-bys on the A165 between the villages of Skirlaugh and Coniston. Uniformed and undercover officers from Humberside Police, responding to complaints from villagers, have been monitoring the lay-bys for a month and during a number of swoops almost twenty people were stopped. But not arrested; it appears that no offences had been committed. In the spirit of our times, the officers resorted to distributing leaflets giving guidance rather than escorting them to the bridewell.

There may have been sound operational reasons why officers were deployed in this way, covertly observing during hours of darkness and out of season what I imagine are little used lay-bys on the road from Hull to Bridlington, but you would have thought they would have had some idea that criminality was involved. The fact that they had taken leaflets along suggests that they thought not, but went to have a look anyway.

Local councillors were not slow in spotting an opportunity to puff out their chests and exercise their pomposity. One East Riding County Councillor thundered, "These public areas have been stolen from the community by individuals in a way they were never intended" (sic). Moreover, one of the lay-bys "is a popular picnic spot". I wonder what he means by the community? Not, surely, the villagers who are unlikely to use the lay-bys. There are lay-bys near to where I live, which I've never used, though I understand that they are popular with fly tippers. People trying to get to Bridlington, perhaps, or families looking for likely spot to get out the Primus and enjoy a cuppa? I'm no expert on dogging, in fact I hardly know what it means, but I have heard that people who dog prefer to do it under cover of darkness, usually after the pubs have closed. Any family caught having a picnic, after dark, on a lay-by on the Bridlington road would probably justify, in the case of the parents, sectioning under the Mental Health Act and their children being rounded up by social services.

Until recently, when a friend's elderly mother announced that dogging is rife in Huddersfield, I had assumed that the practice was confined to the Home Counties. Is Northamptonshire a Home County? If so it will come as no surprise when I tell you that in the village of Hannington the activity is so popular that the local council is attaching supplies of prophylactics to trees so that dogging afficionados can help themselves. Health and Safety, as ever, to the fore; your council taxes at work.

I hope I have not shocked you, but it is as well that you are aware of the dangers that lie in wait if you decide to have a run out to the coast. Remember: the A165 to Bridlington. Gentlemen, start your engines!

Slice of real-life idiocy

In its early days *Private Eye* ran serious investigative journalism alongside spoof articles, and many people complained that they couldn't tell one from the other and, frustrated by their own stupidity, stopped reading the magazine.

Now reality has so far caught up with the *Eye's* ludicrous fantasies that its editorial emphasis has shifted even more onto serious journalism. Humorous invention cannot compete with real life idiocy, much of it displayed by officials. Let me give you a couple of examples, both taken from the same issue of the *Daily Telegraph*.

Eric Pickles last year issued a statutory code requiring local councils to publish details (including job descriptions) of staff earning more than £58,200 a year, and of those spending more than £500. Not surprisingly, many councils have refused to comply – the resistance coming almost certainly from those on the high salaries.

But what is interesting is the excuses they have offered for their delinquency. "So many in this category it would be too onerous to comply" (Kensington and Chelsea, revealingly); "Taxpayers would struggle to assess value for money" (Essex County Council, showing contempt for the voters); "Staff safety could be put at risk if the public knew how much they were paid" (Nottingham, where no-one has wondered why, when GPs, head teachers and senior police officers are not beaten up in the street by furious citizens, pen pushers might be. Or maybe they know.); "There is little public interest in seeing how money is spent" (Knowsley, an astonishing assertion based, one presumes, not on evidence but on casual contempt).

All good, self-serving stuff, as you would expect. But my favourite came from Leeds City Council: "Releasing information could breach intellectual property rights". We are used to the Data Protection Act being cited, inappropriately, as a reason for concealing embarrassing truths, and Health and Safety legislation invoked foolishly, to the fury of those for whom it is a serious concern. These laws are a handy refuge for knaves and those self-important "managers" in their cheap suits, but it is the first time I have heard copyright and patent laws deployed in the interests of official secrecy.

What sort of pond life are they hiring in Leeds City Hall if they seriously think that someone's salary is intellectual property? Do these people even understand what they are saying? An even better question, are they earning more than £58,200 a year? Salaries is private information, and I can understand people being lukewarm about the idea of theirs being published, but public sector pay scales have for generations been in the public domain. If you really want to know what lance corporals or majors in the army are paid, or hospital consultants, or head teachers, the information is readily available. What is not, of course, is where any individual sits on the scale. So, just publish scales and job titles without names. It would be of great interest to taxpayers, even in Essex, to know roughly what "Gender Outreach Officers" and "Climate Change Managers are trousering every year. But that might lead to questions about what they do. I suspect that our man in Leeds has confused copyright law with data protection.

Which brings me to the second *Daily Telegraph* report. Councillors in Gloucestershire have called for a ban on Northerners moving to the South, particularly to Cheltenham, because they expect to live in houses, which are in short supply. That anyone in his right mind should think that such a measure is even possible strains credulity. They'll be building asylum seekers' centres on the racecourse next, to incarcerate those desperate northerners who manage to swim across the Trent and make it to Cheltenham. Or maybe their real fear is that jobseekers from Leeds City Hall, when they have finally been rumbled, might show up looking for work.

Those Were the Days....

I was sorry to hear that the District Council has given notice to quit to the Malton Rifle and Pistol Club to quit its premises on the

Wentworth Street car park. I am not a member of this club; indeed, it might fairly be said that were I to become one, a lapse of judgement on someone's part would have to be involved, an urgent review of the laws governing the use of firearms would be in order. It has a long history, going back four generations, and it is no inward-looking association of shooting enthusiasts. It does good work, for example, in encouraging and coaching teenagers in their pursuit of Duke of Edinburgh Awards, and brings on talent among its members such that some represent Yorkshire in competitive shooting.

It may surprise you to know, I am surprised myself when I think about it, that I was a Duke of Edinburgh Award holder and, almost as impressive, a Queen's Scout. To become a Queen's Scout it was necessary to complete many tasks, physical and intellectual. By far the trickiest was to climb a tree, light a fire up there, boil a billy can of water, make tea and deliver it to the District Commissioner of Scouts who, waiting on the ground, was obliged to drink it. I got the badge, he got the dysentery. It was men (and women, but they were for the Brownies) like him who nurtured and guided spotty, rudderless city youths like me towards purposeful lives and away from the temptations of the streets. This selfless work continues to this day with men and women such as the members of the Rifle and Pistol Club quietly mentoring the next generation. Well, not so quietly, given that firearms are discharged. I suppose they are part of David Cameron's Big Society, but don't mention it to them, they might stop doing it.

I was drawn into talking about life in the fifties and sixties by a dinner companion of about my vintage, one of those tedious people who like nothing better that to look back on a supposed golden age when we were all salt of the earth, manfully (am I allowed this word, Ed?) coping with post-war hardships, making our own entertainment and proud of our integrity. It's not quite how I remember it; certainly there were hardships, but I don't remember being aware of them, though they existed as I can now see. My parents did the coping. There is nothing golden about outside toilets, food rationing, and integrity is not the first word to come to mind when thinking about people routinely robbing off the docks, an activity of which I was only too aware.

In what I consider to be an inspired conversational tactic I managed to force a change of subject by recounting how my sister and I would creep up on my sleeping grandmother and peel the corn plasters off her toes, an inexpensive alternative to Wrigley's Spearmint gum. My companion was chewing a bit of squid at the time. Suddenly she was receptive to a bit of chat about the intellectual nourishment to be had from afternoon telly. I noticed that she started to hide bits of squid, which had clearly lost its charm, under her spinach.

I do not recommend, by the way, making tea up a tree, which in any case is almost certainly illegal now, involving as it does violating numerous Health and Safety regulations with which it is impossible to comply. My advice is, get yourself a decent kettle and boil it in the kitchen, but only after the kettle has been thoroughly checked by a qualified electrician who, if there are any children about, must hold a current CRB certificate. The same goes for the District Commissioner of Scouts if there's one about who looks in need of refreshment.

I gather that the Rifle and Pistol Club has been offered alternative accommodation in a residential area, which is no doubt a neat solution on paper. This will give the residents ample opportunity to discover what it is like to relax of an evening in Beirut. That's the Council for you – working to serve the community. Never mind the fabric, feel the Tesco.

Chicks and carbon rule

My proposal to set up an Old Malton (seniors) Chapter of Hell's Angels has been well received. A former biker chick, Sue Cuthbert, wrote at once applying for membership. It was never my intention to restrict membership to Old Malton residents, even if, like Sue, applicants live in the badlands beyond Pickering. Chicks with experience are especially welcome. Once Sue has successfully met the initiation requirements (hurling an axe twenty-five yards, and holding a wad of rubbing tobacco in the cheek for at least a day) she will be enrolled – petrol head to battery head in two easy stages. I see her already as Head Moll.

I was in Morrison's choosing a shampoo when I was approached by an anxious looking fellow who wanted to know if I had worked through the carbon footprint implications of my plan. Of course I had not. We are to be the lords of disorder, not sandal wearing greens with ambitions to keep a goat or two out the back. In any case, the more I hear about carbon the more confused I become.

Only this week, as I carefully stitched a skull and crossbones onto the back of my linen-cotton mix jacket in front of the telly, I was distracted by a very serious young man who was urging a couple and their two young children to calculate the carbon-cost of the food before buying. In addition to checking out the salt, sugar and fat (saturated and unsaturated) content, and not forgetting the traffic lights, we must, he said, figure out the carbon. This is not a simple matter. A bottle of milk, for example, is the carbon equivalent of travelling a mile on a train, a mixed grill five miles. I am no statistician, but I do wonder about the sums underlying such assertions. Does the train have two carriages or four? Am I the only passenger?

He seemed to be very concerned about the flatulence of cows, and very knowledgeable about it. Cows, I gathered, suffer mightily from flatulence because they have several stomachs, and they express it not, as I had supposed, from the back end but from the front. There was some helpful footage showing a cow with a sort of breathalyser strapped to its head and a pipe disappearing down its throat. I hope that the RSPCA are looking into this. You never hear the carbon evangelists exercising themselves about the flatulence of termites as a result of which a giant pall of carbon hovers constantly over Africa (only Labradors are worse but thankfully there are fewer of them.) This is because I don't eat termites and cannot therefore be blamed – it's the allocation of blame that keeps the zealots so cheerful. What would make them really happy is if we all committed suicide, but we can't do this until carbon capture technology is installed in all crematoria. Anyway, termites are worse than Richard Branson he will be glad to hear. There's no logic to any of this; a banana shipped from South America is more benign, carbon-wise, than a bunch of asparagus grown in Sheriff Hutton because a banana has a thick skin. Well, luckily so have I.

But back to the Hell's Angels. There will have to rules by which members will have to abide, the most important of which are the grounds for expulsion; there are three: 1. Persistently introducing boring guests to join us on rides, 2. Dissing the Head Moll and 3. Cheeking police motorcyclists. The reason for this last is that they are, like us, rockers at heart; they are hiding in the closet until retirement when, once their oily fists have a firm grip on that pension book, they'll be up Old Malton swinging their axes and ready to go. They are the next generation.

You will be wondering how I got on picking out a shampoo best suited to my hair, that day in Morrison's. What was it to be? Extra body and bounce, laboratory tested fly-away formula, or active anti-colour fade ingredients? As I pondered these difficult choices I noticed the prices. I legged it at once down to Yates's and bought some of their own-brand washing up liquid. It comes in gallon cans, cuts through the grease a treat and is competitively priced.

A splendid occasion

I attended this year's Malton Town Council Civic service at St Mary's Priory Church in Old Malton. This is not the sort of event I am usually drawn to, but as the Mayor, Jason Fitzgerald-Smith, is a loyal member of my Wednesday morning breakfast club I felt that I should put in an appearance. You never can tell what sort of a gate you are going to get on these occasions, and I didn't have far to go.

I could not have been more astonished when I arrived. The place was packed with higher-ups; nobs, nabobs and Pooh-Bahs representing every walk of life as far as the eye could see. Dignitaries is not the word. Politicians from every level, high-end pen pushers, freemen of the towns, the suave Fitzwilliam factor, all jockeying for position, seeing and being seen, with a sprinkling of titled personages among them, I shouldn't wonder. All dolled up to the nines, too, in sharp suits and beautiful gowns, none of which could compete with the gorgeous vestments of the master of ceremonies, Canon Manchester, whose golden cope was a temptation to the covetous among us.

I haven't seen, not since the coronation anyway, so many clergy-men milling about in one place. I tried to count them but at five I became drowsy and had to refresh myself by turning to the Book of Common Prayer by reviewing the Table of Kindred and Affinity, an outmoded document if the PM has his way. Apart from canons and curates we had a dean, from whose sermon we discovered the trick of tearing up a telephone directory, and a rural dean, both of senior churchmen. Later, a member of the congregation, who must have heard of my familiarity with matters ecclesiastical, asked me what is the difference between a dean plain and simple, and a rural dean. I have to say that decanal ranking is not my strong suit, but quick as a flash it came to me: a dean lives in a palace whereas a rural dean lives in a field. Not many people know that.

Nor have I seen so many gold chains of office at one go, and I was fearful that the metal thieves might have got wind of our plans. My fears were allayed by the sight of the Chief Constable who, steely eyed, was scanning the crowd for wrong-uns, ready to pounce.

Apart from the excellent sermon on conjuring tricks, the service could not have been better devised and conducted. After a rousing introduction provided by a pair of trumpeters we had familiar hymns sung to familiar tunes, interspersed with prayers of thanks for the good work of the VIPs in the reserved seats who, judging from their serene faces, thought this only right and proper.

Two things stood out for me personally. The first two lines of the final hymn – *The day thou gavest, Lord is ended, / the darkness falls at thy behest* – took me right back to infant school in the fifties when, every Friday afternoon before leaving, we had classroom prayers and sang this hymn, my first experience of pleasure at the arrival of weekends. But above all things I enjoyed the two-handed recitation of a poem given by Lewis Rawling and Bryony Hall, Head Boy and Deputy Head Girl of Malton School. Public performance of poetry is difficult, and they did it splendidly. I spotted Rob Williams, their Headmaster, as ever donnish and grave, looking on, his early anxiety turning visibly to pride as a he saw that they had cracked it.

After the service an exclusive Vesta curry supper had been laid on at a ritzy local eatery; the grandees moved smartly towards their cars, eager to get to the trough. I observed to Mrs Croft that I thought they would be getting a bit tipsy later on but, as she knowingly remarked, I have no room to talk. No invitation for me this year; but that's what exclusive means – keeping out the riff raff.

Decidedly a splendid occasion, which I enjoyed top hole. More grease to your elbow, Mr Mayor.

Nanny's got it covered

The Department of Health has announced a new strategy to support further action by family doctors to reduce our alcohol consumption, based on data from the recently published Screening and Intervention Programme for Sensible Drinking (wittily dubbed SIPS). This new strategy will involve giving extra money to doctors routinely to interrogate us about our drinking habits whenever they come into contact with us.

There appears to be concern about those, like me, of riper years, who are inclined to litter our town centres with broken Zimmer frames and prostheses when they fall over drunk and have to be transported at public expense to A&E departments where fighting invariably breaks out.

We are not aware, they say, of the risks of overdoing it. Even couples who routinely share a bottle of wine over dinner most evenings, they go on, are unwittingly increasing their health risks. These are most unlikely claims. The health warnings about drinking are so frequent and lurid that only those living on another planet can be unaware of the Government's views on the matter. But is an attractive picture they paint, of couples, well on in years, drinking themselves insensible as they share a bottle of Shiraz in the evening. But not one you will see at our house: Mrs Croft insists on having her own bottle.

This interrogation by the doctor, when you pop in for a chat about your shingles or unreliable bladder, will, if you show "signs of high use", be followed by a ten-minute session with a counsellor and/ or referral to a specialist. They call this "opportunist detection"; I call it meeting trouble half way. And it is expensive, doctors' time costing what it does. Much better would be a system, modelled on the Neighbourhood Watch scheme, whereby volunteer members of the community could be recruited to rat on each other to the authorities who could then pounce and haul the offending bibbers off to secure accommodation for enforced detoxification.

Of course, there would be those who would use this as an opportunity to settle old scores, as the East German Stasi discovered; everyone would have a little list. This would keep us on our toes, and could have its benefits; if all those having a grievance with a neighbour about a privet hedge were to be hauled off for forcible detoxification they would not be available to clog up the courts with trivial litigation, freeing up the criminal justice to deal with more serious matters, such as people expressing theological reservations about same-sex marriage or the social habits of the Welsh.

What the pointy-heads at the Department of Health seem to have overlooked is the role of Government as a cause of this epidemic of reckless drinking among pensioners. Denied access to euthanasia, and increasingly under attack by their friends at the Treasury, we are becoming depressed about a future in which we see no alternative but to turn off the heating, skip meals and drink ourselves to death with highly taxed booze.

There are of course some benefits in cutting back on the drinking, one of which I observed recently in a clever economist friend of mine. After a few months working in the Middle East, with no access at all to alcohol, he returned a changed man. He had been of a build best described as well upholstered, or as my mother used to say well covered – "you know who I mean," she would say, "she's that well-covered woman who lives next door to her who lost a leg to sugar diabetes". Anyway, he came back well slimmed down and has taken to swaggering about in clothes he has not been able to get into for decades. He showed up at a curry lunch in a nifty charcoal grey suit, beautifully cut in a style that, given time, may well come back. *Bella figura* is the term. I won't name him (he's a shy man), but if you spot a chap who resembles an un-guyed wigwam, that'll be him in old outfit.

Bottoms up!

Obituaries

I read the obituaries and death notices every day, and I am seldom disappointed. It is, I suppose, a symptom of advancing years, this curiosity about the deaths of one's acquaintances – a Gothic taste enjoyed by those who are, as junior doctors say, "circling the drain". I make no claims that there is anything especially healthy about this preoccupation, but there are some benefits; for a start it enables efficient thinning out of the Christmas card list, which with the cost of a stamp shortly to rise to twelve shillings is no small consideration. Not that it works particularly well, what with newcomers insinuating themselves into one's affections and the next generation bloating the list by their hectic breeding programmes, and the older generation clinging on like limpets to their spots on the Christmas card list as they go for the ton.

My generation is caught in a demographic perfect storm of longevity, fecundity and felonious raids on our pensions mounted by wealthy toffs in the Cabinet. I told Mrs Croft some years ago to accept no further invitations to social functions as I took the view that I had more than enough friends, many of them of an unsatisfactory sort, some of them downright unsavoury. But her enthusiasm for inspecting the domestic arrangements of others has stubbornly overwhelmed common sense with the result that, against all expectations, one keeps running into people one likes, and every time that happens it's twelve bob down the drain in December, just for the postage, and every December thereafter. But why on earth, I hear you cry, don't you buy second class stamps? Because Mrs Croft believes that if people think we can't afford first class they won't want to be our friends. You see my problem.

Why does it cost twelve shillings to send a greetings card to Pickering, where of course I have heaps of chums? The GPO says it is because they have to deliver to Thurso in the winter and the cost of compensating postmen who are bitten by bad tempered polar bears puts a significant strain on the overheads, though I doubt if this is true. Just this week I received a letter from America and I happened to notice, as I checked to see if the franking machine had missed the stamp, that it had cost $1.05 – at current exchange rates about twelve shillings. This letter had been carried from central Pennsylvania to an airport, probably Philadelphia, then flown over three thousand miles to London to be sorted and secured by a red rubber band for the trip to Malton for delivery by our own posties. What is more, it contained a cheque for a thousand dollars, not something you see every day and a better return than I have ever seen from a Christmas card.

I see no way out of this fix. A friend told me once, rather morosely, that the only way of making sure that your wife never leaves you is to murder her, but it does defeat the object of the exercise. Cutting down the Christmas card list on this principle would be a much greater challenge; the benefits would be better defined, but even a slow witted probationary constable would spot a sinister cluster of violent deaths in Old Malton before much headway had been made, and fingers would inevitably be pointed, followed by the inevitable dawn swoop.

So there it is, something for us all to think about. Suggestions on a postcard, please – at current prices it'll cost you less than ten bob.

But I didn't say anything...

You probably imagine that I spend all my time arched over a hot typewriter laboriously bashing out six hundred words of rubbish with a few choice remarks about local nobs mixed in. You would be right, but last week was different. I was summoned to New York, all expenses paid, to attend a high level meeting at the headquarters of Home Box Office (HBO).

Why, I hear you ask, and why me? It is a little known fact that I write for *Collier's* magazine, a bi-monthly descendant of *Collier's Weekly*, which before its demise in the sixties enjoyed a circulation of three million and the services of such writers as Mark Twain, Ernest Hemingway and Winston Churchill. The magazine has nothing to do with coal mining, by the way. Coincidentally, HBO have just completed a feature film, *Hemingway and Gellhorn*, directed by Philip Kaufman (*The Unbearable Lightness of Being, The Right Stuff, Raiders of the lost Ark*, the list goes on). Martha Gellhorn, who was Hemingway's third wife, is played by Nicole Kidman. She was a distinguished war correspondent who wrote for *Collier's Weekly*. Hemingway is played by Clive Owen, a British actor. I was wanted at the meeting, they said, to bring some British gravitas to the proceedings. Never before has the word gravitas been used in a sentence that included a reference to me, which is fair enough, but it was unnecessary I thought for Mrs Croft repeatedly to point this out.

The meeting began with a viewing of the film in a private theatre on whose plush seats many plump and self-important bottoms have reposed over the years, followed by a two-hour symposium with the director. The film, which will be released in May, is excellent, marred only by Miss Kidman's tendency to remove her clothes on any and every pretext. I found this upsetting, but I didn't say anything. Before all this, I should add, the proprietor of *Collier's* gave me a box of five hundred business cards on which I was styled "Foreign Correspondent", an unexpected promotion, but they were taken away from me before I caught my 'plane home. I didn't say anything.

The days following the HBO summit meeting were taken up entirely with boosting the revenues of the California wine industry by enthusiastically consuming their product in the company of a number of rowdy Americans, some of them claiming to know me. The hospitality was, as it always is in America, outstandingly generous; the ribs and steaks were excellent, the wines flowed freely.

On the flight home I noticed a number of oddballs, as Americans call them. There was a woman wearing a tangerine backpack that exactly matched the colour of her hair, and a gent in bib and brace overalls and a stained trilby, obviously a share cropper who had mistaken our Boeing 747 for a Greyhound bus. But my favourite, sitting right next to me, was a man in his eighties who, once the 'plane began to move, put on a crash helmet which he removed only when we had reached cruising altitude. During the flight he read with furious concentration a book called *Valuables in the Attic*, underlining those passages that most caught his eye. On every page only two or three lines remained un-highlighted. It occurred to me that it would have been more efficient to have underlined only those lines that were of no interest, but I didn't say anything. When our pilot announced that we were about to begin our descent into Heathrow, oddball put away his book and strapped on his crash helmet again in preparation for landing. Both a pessimist and an optimist.

During the meal (which I refused – it looked vile) he told me that he was on his way to enjoy a four week cycling holiday in Holland and that his bike, a Rudge Gent's I bet, was safely stowed in the hold. I suppose when you are eighty and cycling up hills gets difficult, Holland is the best spot to head for, but it did occur to me that it would be cheaper for him to buy a moped and stay at home. I didn't say anything. As we prepared to disembark, or deplane as they say, he put on his cycle clips. I hope he is enjoying his holiday. Certainly, he'll fit right in among the Dutch.

Did I mention it was an all expenses paid trip? *Mercury* editor please note, I fancy an outing to Brid.

Preparation for winter challenge

In only a couple of weeks or so the days will begin to shorten, the evenings draw in and our minds will turn to winter preparations.

I shall be bobbing down to Yates's to buy a new puncture outfit so that I can do some running repairs on my wellies, which have sprung a few leaks over the summer. What is it about puncture outfits, that the glue goes off after a single use? And why has no-one come up with one that includes self-adhesive patches? The biggest dividend of the American space programme was the quantum leap in the quality of adhesives, which we see daily in the envelopes we buy and in the confidence we now feel in dental crowns, and yet we still have to fiddle about with tubes of glue and French chalk when mending a puncture.

But more important than leaky wellies, we must prepare for the challenges to our health that winter brings; mysterious agues that baffle the doctor ("it seems to be going around at the moment"), unpleasant viruses and dangerous bacilli. Gone are the days when we could give the children a good covering of goose fat and sew them into their underwear until the spring. Ours is a more scientific age, goose fat is expensive and that Esther Rantzen is always ready to pounce.

Make a diary note to start pestering the Derwent Practice for your 'flu jabs as soon as the schools go back in September. My mother had a particular autumnal concern about rheumatic fever, and she knew what to about it: ensure that the whole family dry between their toes after taking a bath. Her parting words to me when, dry-eyed and eager, she pushed me onto the platform at Hull's Paragon Station to get the train to university, were "And don't forget to dry between your toes". No fancy streptococcal theories for her.

Not all prophylactic measures and remedies need to be evidence based, no matter what our doctors claim; medical advice changes weekly, but old wives' tales last for ever, so hang on to your favourites. I recently discovered that an old friend holds an unshakeable belief in the power of higher education to protect against a wide range of ailments, especially those giving rise to gastro-intestinal uproar such as winter vomiting disease (WVD). Unfortunately, according to him, it only works if you have a PhD, which I don't. I was struck down by WVD last winter and jolly unpleasant it was and I am keen to avoid a repetition. My son, Edward, has one but when I asked if I could borrow it for the winter, he flat out refused, which I thought was a bit much seeing as I had financed it. Said he would be using it himself.

However, all is not lost. I have discovered that you can, for a few dollars, purchase a doctorate of your choice from any number of obscure universities located in the Deep South of America. I shall be investing in a nifty Doctor of Science degree in the confident expectation that I shall sail through winter untroubled by ghastly ailments. With the dual protection of an evidence-based 'flu jab and a dodgy certificate from Louisiana I can set all my worries aside. And remember, the 'flu jab lasts for only a year, but the DSc is a lifetime deal. I wonder if I can get the NHS to stump up for it.

All of which reminds me of our personnel manager in Nigeria. He was very fond of talking about his London University doctorate, but after a time I became suspicious, especially when he told me that he had never had a passport, and asked to see the certificate. He tried to fob me off with a scruffy photocopy but I demanded the original, which turned out to be an obvious forgery. That was the end of him. I do remember that he was off work a lot with malaria, and now I know why. If he had written to Louisiana and stumped a few dollars he could have had the genuine article and kept his health. And his job. This is quality advice you're getting here.

Drones amid the Jubilee parties

The Old Malton Jubilee street party was a great success, thanks to the efforts of innumerable worker bees under the direction of Queen Bee Betty Smith and many extraordinarily generous donors. There were of course the usual drones (the economist and myself chief among them). We had a rollicking good time, with Dave Sawdon at the turntable doing a Hank Wangford impersonation as MC.

There was a Victoria sponge competition, possibly the key event, and I was a contender. I am not much of a cake eater, and I had certainly never previously baked one, but I thought it was time for an outsider, a rank outsider some say, to give the goodwives of Old Malton a master class in deft cookery. For too long they have rested on their laurels. And how difficult can it be? Not very is the answer, not for an intuitive cook such as myself. I did a dry run on the day before but the result, although outstanding and probably a game-changer, was not quite perfect so I tweaked the recipe and made a second run at it early on Tuesday morning.

When I placed my cake on the table among the other entries I had a quick look at them, and at once scented victory and fancied myself the winner, especially when I noticed among them a few carrot cakes and lemon drizzle cakes. Why would anyone do that? It's a bit like entering a Gloucester Old Spot in the toy poodle category at Cruft's. Anyway, I could see it coming – I would be declared "victor ludorum summa cum laude" before the day was out. No need to attempt to corrupt the judges, which was just as well as Rev. Ian Robinson was among them, a man not easily bent out of shape.

I was stunned when the result, the incomprehensible result, was announced – I had come fourth. Fourth! Had there been a fix? Not very likely, not in Old Malton, but as a close student of the Archers I know that such things are not unknown. Or had word reached the judges that I had, the week before, propositioned Andrew, the excellent baker at The Patisserie on Newbiggin, to bake for me a Plan B cake that I could, in the event that Mrs Croft slammed a door when my own effort was in the oven, slip in as my own. Perhaps the judges, noting the incomparable quality of my cake, had concluded that it could only have been baked by a professional pastry chef, that I must have entered a ringer and discounted me. They were not necessarily to know that he had flat out refused, denouncing the whole idea as unethical, whatever that means. Well, he's a man of integrity is what it means, I know that now. Such was my bitterness at not winning I could not even try a slice of my own product – it would have brought the bile to my throat. I consoled myself with several glasses of wine, kindly offered to me by the only medical man present, who, seeing my state, knew exactly what to prescribe.

Apart from the infamous cake competition, the whole day went very well. Lots of children, far too much food, side shows, and tough-looking ton-up merchants on big bikes boosting our spirits by honking and waving to us as they passed. A very happy conclusion to a remarkable weekend of national celebrations of HMQ's sixty years on the throne.

I can report one odd episode, which occurred just as things were winding down. A retired colonel of my acquaintance was spotted at the road side, one trouser leg rolled up and holding aloft a tray of iced fancies, gesturing with winsome smiles at passing cars. It was far from clear what his intentions were; was he trying to off-load surplus buns, or hitch a lift to the bus station? I noticed that his bizarre blandishments resulted only in cars putting on a burst of speed as soon as they saw him. An odd business, I think you'll agree.

Popping down to see the family

Last Friday I went South to visit my daughter who wanted me to go with her to Addenbrooke's Hospital in Cambridge where she had an appointment for a scan.

She is seven months pregnant. She is taking part in a research programme called POP, as in Pregnancy Outcome Prediction study, nothing to do with being "about to pop" though I expect the boffins were very pleased with their little joke. I have seen this pre-natal imaging before, but never in real time involving someone close to me. Spooky.

At first it was difficult to make sense of what I was seeing; it was a bit like looking at satellite images of a hurricane moving up the Gulf of Mexico.

But, guided by the operator, who was a good teacher as well as clever technician, I eventually got the hang of it and was able to see the anatomical features of my granddaughter-to-be who, in no time at all will doubtless be manipulating me just as her mother did - still does, actually - and with the same ski-slope nose, I noticed. I recommend the experience if you get the chance. I also noticed that in the imaging unit there were three ladies' loos, signed in pink, but no gents'. What about the anxious fathers and bewildered grandfathers who must from time to time pass through? Pass through, but not pass water evidently. Time for a bit of equality I say.

Back home Mrs Croft and I stayed up to listen to The Archers, as is we do, and when I went to put the milk bottles on the step I noticed a rather suspicious looking character lurking outside, and another like him further along the street. Villains for sure, I thought, casing the joint in preparation for a major heist. They were carrying torches, communicating with each other by walkie-talkies, and wearing day-glow tabards to give them an official air. I was tempted to ring 999, or whatever the number now is, but I strode boldly out, Horlicks in hand, and confronted the blighters.

It was just as well I didn't summon an armed response team from Thirsk; it turned out that they were bat welfare officers, social workers for bats. I assured him that round this way we are very keen on bats, which seemed to please him, but his pleasure quickly turned sour when I added that we prefer them deep-fried, like whitebait. He nervously fiddled with his walky-talky, considering summoning the bat protection SWAT team I suppose, to cork me up in Flamingo Land until a magistrate be found. But then he relaxed, having I concluded, I think, that that he had stumbled upon a lunatic, possibly harmless, recently released into the community; he explained, nervously I thought, that they were counting pipistrelle bats. How? Why? And who is paying for these sinister people to terrorise blameless taxpayers (that's a clue, by the way) by hanging about in the streets at night? I didn't challenge him with these difficult questions, because I know that these bats people have the power to hit you with an enforcement order obliging you to fit out your loft with heaters in case it gets cold and the bats don't like it. I encouraged his evaluation of my mental state by rolling my eyes and shuffling of muttering, "I'm thinking of invading Poland". I think I've all this right, but I had taken my deaf aid out in readiness for bed (not that Mrs Croft snores or anything) and couldn't really hear either of us. The next morning they were gone. I got the chip pan out.

Enough about batty social workers, let's get back to grand children – much more interesting. My grandson Archie, who has just started school was dragooned along with his class mates in that boring way teachers have into making Fathers' Day cards. What's wrong with Hoppers, for goodness' sake? Anyway, he refused and insisted on making instead a Grandfather's Day card, putting on it a crayon depiction of me, adding a beard and omitting a leg. Is he a free-thinker, or has he figured out whose will is likely to be read first? I don't know, but bats he isn't.

Gathering of clan at Irish weekend

Mrs Croft's family, on her father's side, is Irish. Known, years ago, as the "Fighting Foleys", they are now almost entirely respectable; mostly lawyers if that's not a contradiction in terms.

Every two or three years there is a gathering of the clan, either in Ireland or over here. It was such a moot that took us to Surrey and West Sussex last weekend. We drifted in from Dublin, Galway, the West Country, Wales of all places, and of course Yorkshire.

We checked into a hotel, which to my irritation claimed a dubious connection with Charles Dickens; in fact the room we used was called the Charles Dickens Room.

My first reaction was to kick up a bit of a fuss on behalf of Malton about this sly passing-off, but I soon realised there was no point as the place was staffed entirely by Polish speakers.

Perhaps I should get Linda McCarthy on the case, or the Mayor; they look like people who might know a bit of Polish.

Two odd incidents occurred. We were loitering on the hotel steps, waiting for our cab to take us to the ceilidh, when a woman came up to me and tried to give me the keys to her hat shop; had I been lighter on my feet I would have taken them.

Then, blow me down, another woman approached Mrs Croft and said, "I know this is a bit random, but I just want to say how beautifully dressed you are". Random? What can she have meant? Anyway, be warned: avoid Guildford if you can, but if not watch out. Unpredictable people are being released into the community there.

There were three social events, but I missed the second because I was detained elsewhere checking Mrs Croft into a detox clinic for a quick purge.

The thing about the Irish lot is that they devote the same intense dedication to drinking as they did getting themselves qualified as lawyers.

And they can talk, usually all at once, mainly about politics and family history.

Staying up until gone three in the morning drinking furiously, with my hearing aids switched off, is not my usual way at the weekend – in fact I'm generally getting up to walk the dog not long after that. We got back to Yorkshire utterly exhausted.

But no so exhausted that I couldn't call in on the daughter on the way back to make sure she is not overdoing things, being great with child and everything. Not splitting too many logs, that kind of thing.

I'm becoming something of a maven in matters obstetric, and my wise observations on foetal welfare are always well received.

I have discovered that the standard formula for calculating the due date of birth is based on secondary results of research conducted in 1840. Using this method seventy-five percent of babies are "late", of which a third are more than two weeks "late". It is for this reason that goodwives, most of whom are not statisticians, mutter darkly, "They're always late".

Of course, they are not – what happens in the majority of cases is normal. So as a matter of routine no fewer than seventy-five of pregnant women are given something to worry about in the final weeks of pregnancy because we continue to use an early nineteenth century formula that is inaccurate, and what is more, known to be inaccurate.

I confidently predict a September birth, the best month for later educational achievement.

With the Irish weekend now behind us there's not much to look forward to until October.

In spite of my muscular build and athletic, loose-limbed gait I am not much interested in sport.

I am intensely irritated that the BBC is devoting the output of its two main channels exclusively to the Olympics. (There will, however, be brief news summaries each day to let us know which bankers have joined their co-conspirators on remand).

It's all very well pandering to single issue fanatics in this way, but how would they feel if a whole month were to be given over to non-stop Antiques Road Show and Let's Get Baking.

But I console myself that the evenings are drawing in now, and summer will soon be behind us.

Memories of a colourful character

For a few years after I left university I was a schoolmaster, right at the fag-end of the grammar school era when eccentrics were still tolerated in school staff rooms, and it was in one such place that I ran into a very colourful character. He was a Cambridge mathematician who had done spells in the Royal Navy and in industry before going into teaching, quickly becoming deputy headmaster, which is where I found him when I joined the staff as a new teacher.

Unusually, given our distance from each other on the totem pole, we became friends. I cannot now remember why. Certainly it was not in any hope on my part of recruiting an influential friend; he was cordially disliked by the headmaster and most of the teachers, and his social ineptitude was such that he was unable to exercise any influence whatever.

He was a bachelor of about forty, and set in his ways. His ordering of his life was based on logic, and his logic, although immaculate, was invariably based on faulty premises. For example, he was very concerned about efficient use of his time, in pursuit of which it was his habit, before retiring for the night, to treat himself to poached eggs and cornflakes, followed by a shave, so that he could hit the day running the following morning. Presumably this theory was put into practice only after he had left the Navy.

The view from his kitchen window was marred by a tatty structure on a bit of land, a wooden barn in use as a garage, large enough to accommodate several cars and in need of a lick of paint. A Cambridge friend who came to stay commented on this, saying what a pity it was that he overlooked this unsightly structure. As soon as his visitor had gone, he ran out and bought a can of petrol and used it to set fire to the building which quickly took hold and spread to some nearby poplar trees. Neighbours called the fire brigade, and he was visited by the police. It was only when he received a bill from the fire service that I heard about this episode; he came to me in great indignation, asking me how he should respond, and I coaxed the story out of him. He was difficult to advise, so convinced was he that his behaviour had been reasonable, but I did persuade him to pay up. He was not prosecuted.

His most hilarious stunt was to fix himself up with a wig (he was very bald), which he acquired by mail order and fitted himself, showing up at school after spending the half term break practising wearing it. It takes a brave teacher to do this, a move best made, if at all, between jobs in the hope that it will not be noticed by the pupils. The fact that it was differently adjusted each day led to total collapse of his authority, and the last I heard of him he had become a headmaster in Botswana.

One day I sloped off to the staff room for what in those days was known as a free period (non-contact time now), looking forward to a fag and a coffee, and spotted the senior mistress and the games mistress rushing off to deal with a crisis. I found him, looking sour, alone in the staff room and asked him what was going on. There had been, he told me, a case of indecent exposure in the park nearby involving a young girl from the school, which he described as "a lot of fuss about nothing" and when I said I thought it was serious he said, "nonsense, that's what parks are for". This surprised me, and when I pressed him on it I discovered that he didn't know what indecent exposure was, thinking it was merely older men looking at young girls in a funny way (also not what parks are for). I explained it to him, he didn't believe me. I persuaded a more experienced teacher to explain it, who he did believe, whereupon he flew into a rage, loudly advocating public birching for such offenders to anyone who would listen.

I often wonder how he got on in the Navy. While not suggesting that they teach indecent exposure there, I would be surprised if there weren't some jokes about it. He wouldn't have understood them, perhaps, but how could he not know what every schoolboy knows?

Music is grand but an odd business

The house I live in backs onto a 12th century churchyard, which is a very pleasant spot to end up in. The house, I mean, not the churchyard, though I suppose that may also true. Just as I was about to hop into bed one night recently, I heard the sounds of activity, voices and doors banging, coming from the vicinity of the church. Tomb raiders, I thought, or Satanists looking for an atmospheric venue for a bit of sacrilege. I grabbed my Maglite torch, as much an offensive weapon as a source of illumination, and went to explore.

It was at first sight worse than I feared – a white van and a couple of lads from Ashington. I have never been to Ashington, but I once was told that its most attractive features are plastic beer mugs and fading love bites. It'll be the lead on the roof, or off it more likely, that will be the interest. But not a bit of it – they were delivering not taking away, and delivering something more valuable than any lead, a Steinway grand piano for use at the musical concert the following day. They we as surprised by me as I was by them, what with my skinny white legs showing below my dressing gown and naked terror on my face. I stayed and chatted with them as they managed the ton and a half musical instrument out of the van and into position at the front of the church, helped by a huge battery powered trolley.

They finally left well after midnight for a two-hour drive back to Ashington, with the prospect of a six o'clock alarm call to take another piano to a Ryedale Festival location and another musical event. The following day at the concert, which was packed out, I reflected that very few of my fellow music lovers could have been aware of the contribution made to their pleasure by these County Durham movers. Not to mention the more modest contribution of an elderly gent, shivering in a cold church in his nightie, waiting to lock up after them. It's all very well clapping the instrumentalists on the day, but I did think me and Durham boys should have had a round of applause, albeit scattered applause probably.

If you are hoping for a review of the concert, you have come to the wrong place. No-one has ever accused me of being a musical person, especially not my music master, the saintly but sadly asthmatic Mr "Wheezy" Graydon, who diagnosed my tone deafness at our first meeting. I will say this, however: the concert had the merit of being short, a little over an hour. As Winston Churchill said, "The mind will not absorb more than the bottom can endure"; the pews in St Mary's were designed to test fundamental endurance, I suppose to discourage snoozing during sermons, and I was relieved to get away for a spot of lunch. But I had been delighted for an hour or so and I was grateful to the performers. And of course to the Ashington crew. Now I come to think of it, maybe it was Ashford I'd heard about – it is, after all, in Kent, and just across the river from Essex.

Music is an odd business. We can all run, walk, write, talk and although we may not do these things well we are aware when others do it better because we can do them ourselves, however poorly. For example, I can run and I can talk, but only haltingly; I can however appreciate the superlative achievements of Lord Coe who ran like the wind in his heyday and is only now peaking in the talking department. Music is not like this – if you can't do it, you don't really understand what those who can are really up to. It's a bit like being colour blind; you cannot, by trying harder, see green as other men see it. But you can run faster if you train hard, though not as fast as the Lord Coe naturally.

On the subject of athletics, I have very much enjoyed the world class perversion of English that has been coming out of the mouths of sports commentators. My favourite (so far) is the reference to an outstanding female competitor as a "taliswoman", incorporating as it does a faulty grasp of English as well as foolish political correctness. A possible gold there.

Why Olympics are a saw point...

In an attempt to draw attention away from what has been described as my unmanly disdain for the Olympics I have acquired a bench saw, also known as a mitre saw. This has involved a thorough reorganisation of the garage, including, but not limited to, re-wiring it, a skill not usually associated with a temperament like mine. "Why is it", says Mrs Croft, "that whenever you bring such an article into the house everything has to be upside down?". I thought, but didn't say, that the same could be said about some of the more ambitious projects undertaken in the kitchen.

Such saws are not a trivial purchase. Initial research revealed that I would have to part with a sum greater than I have ever given for a good suit (i.e. £200); more thought was needed. What about second hand? After a deal of rooting about I found just the item in a pawn shop in Scarborough at the knock down price of forty quid, and it came with a seven-day guarantee. You can't turn your back on a snip like that, and besides, where can you get a suit for forty quid these days? Nor have I ever been given a guarantee with a suit, not even a new one.

Why I might need such a piece of equipment is less easily explained than how I came to acquire one. At our house we enjoy the benefit of a wood burning stove, got up in a tasteful maroon specially picked out by Mrs Croft, which we fire up not only in the interests of keeping warm but also to reduce our climate footprint, a vital consideration. The price of logs, like everything else, continues to rise and I have taken up totting as we called it when I was a child. So successful have I been in this enterprise that I have accumulated a considerable quantity of timber, most of which needs cutting down to fit in the stove. I have only limited capability with a hand saw because of an infirmity in my right shoulder caused, not by shrapnel that could not safely be removed, a claim I sometimes make, but possibly by fifty years of hoisting large wine goblets to my lips, an unkind diagnosis confidently made by my cynical children but not confirmed by my physician.

It took me a while to get the saw secured to the bench, with power laid on, by which time it was Day Eight and the guarantee had run out, when of course I discovered a fault with the foolproof guard mechanism. The problem turned out to be a design flaw, but after hours of fiddling and adjusting I overcame it and went into production. I have to say, it's a beautiful thing, and with winter bearing down on us a thing I have urgent need of. A useful little feature is a bag that collects some sawdust, but not all. This comes in very handy whenever I want to slope off to read cheap fiction and eat toffees: I scatter sawdust about and when Mrs Croft asks why I have not cut the grass/oiled the gate/bathed the dog I can point to the evidence of my manly endeavours on the garage floor.

But, back to the Olympics. I was mystified when we made our bid, and appalled when we succeeded. My worst fears have been realised: mounting costs, disgusting pandering to the "Olympic Family" with Zil lanes and free rooms in top hotels, and hanging over it all a whiff of corruption. The sanctimonious hope expressed by all those sucking on the five ring lobster, that the "lasting legacy" universal indulgence organised physical jerks can be guaranteed to put paid to the obesity epidemic is a con. Their smugness is exceeded only by their cynicism in partnering with manufacturers of notoriously unhealthy fast food, chocolate and sugary drinks. Be prepared to witness a boost to our position in the international obesity league tables, but I hope a boost in the medal tables.

Such is the power of these junk food sponsors that hundreds of uniformed jobsworths are now on the streets threatening £20,000 fines to anyone who seeks to associate his business with The Games.

Woe betide any butcher who, even inadvertently, so arranges Cumberland sausages on his trays that they may call to mind the five sacred rings. Worst of all, amid the security mess being swiftly addressed by police and military personnel called in at the eleventh hour we hear that the rent-a-cop brigade have the impertinence to try to issue them with orders.

Luckily, the uniforms have the good sense to tell them, with great civility I don't doubt, where to stuff it.

Thoroughbred was a racing certainty

Quite by chance, I stumbled on an interesting story. I was walking down Old Maltongate on my way to collect my car from the Talbot Hotel car park, abandoned there the previous evening after over-enthusiastically refreshing myself at dinner, and I ran into Claire Waltham. We know each other from walking our dogs by the Derwent, and we stopped for a chat. I was planning to go to York Races later that day and I mentioned this; she told me that her late grandfather was a jockey called Billy Bullock who had won the

Epsom Derby and the Epsom Oaks in the same year, 1908.

When I got home I mentioned this story to Tim Hailstone, an old friend who was staying with us, also bound for York Races, who is very knowledgeable about racing; he knew about Billy Bullock's remarkable achievement. Not only did he win the Derby, and two days later the Oaks, but he did it on the same horse, the only rider ever to have done so. The horse was called Signorinetta.

Signorinetta was a British Thoroughbred racehorse and broodmare which in a short racing career from 1907 to 1908 ran thirteen times, and won three races – two of them Classics, the Derby and the Oaks. She was bred, owned and trained by an eccentric Italian called Edoardo Ginistrelli. Signorinetta's dam was Signorina, who had been unbeaten in nine races as a two-year-old, won twice the following season, and was runner up in the Epsom Oaks.

At the same Newmarket stables was an undistinguished stallion, Chaleureux, whose only function was to be a "teaser", that is to detect when broodmares come into season for the information of better qualified suiters. Ginistrelli noticed that whenever Chaleureux passed Signorina's box he would whinny to her; from this he concluded that the animals were in love and he allowed them to mate. To allow a prize mare to breed from an unrated stallion would, in horse-breeding circles, be viewed as an unwise decision, but Ginistrelli justified it on the "boundless laws of sympathy and love".

Well, that's Italians for you. A foal was in due course produced – Signorinetta, whose place in racing history has not been matched in over a hundred years. In the Derby she started at odds of 100/1. Lord Alfred Douglas, famously Oscar Wilde's catamite, placed a bet of £5 to win and collected the equivalent of over £40,000 in today's money. I wonder if Bosey slipped Willy Bullock a fiver? I hope so.

Which brings us back to the Ebor and my day's betting.

Like Lord Alfred Douglas, my preferred stake is £5 (the only preference we share), and this is what I placed on all six races. I have a very simple system: I back only horses that have been trained in Malton, a system that has served me very well in the past. I call it the Easterby-Fahey formula.

I usually bet each way, but this year, fuelled by alcohol and driven by greed, I played only to win. The results were catastrophic – thirty quid down the drain. You may think that I am tempted to blame Mr Easterby and Mr Fahey for my disappointing day, but the truth is that if I had followed my usual practice and placed each way bets I would have gone home with my finances in a rather less ruinous state.

What with reckless betting and dinner at the Talbot it was a costly week, but worth it – even with the soaking I had in the torrential rain on the course.

Exciting time with arrival of two 'minors'

I am happy to say that my daughter, Helen, has given birth to her first child, a girl, and both are well. She weighed in at 7lbs 13oz and is called Maggie; in the end Howardina didn't cut the mustard.

But the really exiting news is that I have bought a new car. She's a nineteen sixties Morris Minor shooting brake; dark green with wood trim, practically in showroom nick.

This vehicle has been available for a few weeks from Mathewson in Thornton-le-Dale, who posed seductively on the forecourt to catch the eye of a discerning pensioner anxious to reconnect with his past. Actually, my father's past; this is the very model of car that he always wanted, but never had. How I wish I could drive it back forty years and give it to him. Well, let him have a sit in it at least.

It is not in my nature to rush into things, especially where expenditure is involved; I had to mull it over. It tells you something about my cautious way when it comes to parting with money that I spent about the same length of time pondering the purchase of a seven-pack of socks on offer at Marks and Sparks as I did over this car.

The day came when I squired Mrs Croft over to Thornton-le-Dale to inspect and admire this vehicle. I had a long chat with the man at the garage, all about contact points, track rod ends and torque ratios the way real men do, and then went for a spin in her, giving Mrs Croft time to make the final decision. It was a yes!

The test drive was a bit hair-raising. No power steering, long whippy gear stick, enormous steering wheel and, or so I first thought, no brakes. I was told that frequently when people buy such classic cars they bring them back the next day asking how the brakes can be made more effective: the reply is always, press harder on the pedal. It'll take some getting used to – no disc brakes, no power steering, and only the Light Programme and Home Service on the radio, if there is one.

Keep your eyes peeled. You will probably spot me motoring about the district like Mr Toad, waving to surprised and envious fellow citizens, and swaggering up and down beside it in an ecstasy of self-admiration when we are parked up in the Market Place. I am thinking of investing in some string back gloves and a shorty car coat to complete the new image. Bella figura is the phrase that will spring to mind when you see me out and about. Babe magnet or what?

Mrs Croft will be surprised and delighted to receive at Christmas a nifty meths stove, which will enable us stop in lay-bys for a cuppa whenever we feel like one, being careful of course to avoid those notorious East Riding lay-bys frequented by doggers, which I have mentioned before.

Once the deal had been done I applied at once for membership of the East Yorkshire Thoroughbred Car Club, an association of nostalgic petrol heads such as me. Speaking of which, while BP spends millions taking the lead out of petrol I shall bed putting some back in. This car club membership will entitle me to join its summer parade of classic cars from Hull to Bridlington, the highlight of the EYTCC calendar, and give me access to the motoring experience and knowledge of hundreds of chaps in shorty car coats.

Anyway, back to this baby. She was eight days late, so will probably be like her mother who was late for one of her university interviews and turned up on the wrong day for another. She was born at 7.20am, but I didn't hear until 10am so I must have been fairly low down on the list of people to call. One of the pleasing features of this whole business was how much Helen enjoyed being pregnant, but from childhood she has always enjoyed being the centre of attention so several months of it was right up her street.

On the subject of grandchildren, my grandson Archie (5) who is in Year One (which is actually his second year; his first year was Year Zero) has been elected Year Representative by his peers. I don't know what it means. Will he be attending meetings of governors, and sitting on interview panels? Anyway, he is continuing a Croft family tradition of accepting positions of responsibility stretching all the way back to his own father. Maggie will keep up with him, I'm sure.

I decided against the seven-pack of socks, by the way, just in case you are wondering. A bit pricey I thought, and there's the cost of the shorty car coat to consider. Poop Poop!

Pension pots should be left alone

That nice Mr Clegg, I notice, is planning to make pilfering from pensioners part of government policy, rather in the way that not-so-nice Mr Brown did when he was Chancellor of the Exchequer. Ever since my own retirement was in the offing the politicians have been nibbling away at the benefits.

I shall be sorry to see my bus pass go, which it seems certain to do. It's not so much the financial benefit, which may not look much from the back of a ministerial limo though I'm glad of it, but it is useful evidence of age when claiming OAP discounts. Am I challenged about this because people like to be difficult, or because they are misled by my youthful appearance and supple, loping gait? I suspect the latter. Even my own GP, whose "clinical gaze" enables him to spot old bones, asked me if I was still paying for my prescriptions, which means he judges me to be, possibly, a decade younger than I am. Maybe it is part of modern bedside manner – send them away cheerful, but make a note, "Do Not Resuscitate", anyway.

I am also rather attached to my winter fuel allowance, which arrives in my account just before Christmas; the moment it arrives I run down to my man in Norton and blow the lot on festive wine which, with any luck, will keep me warm into January.

It is difficult to see how these "reforms", which will involve some form of means testing, will yield much of a saving. I suspect that many people who, like me, can afford to run a car make only occasional use of the bus pass, the confiscation of which would provide only trivial economies. But the entire population of current bus pass holders would have to be screened to pick those from whom passes would be seized, with routine means testing of all applicants thereafter. The cost of the necessary army of jobsworths to do all this will surely exceed any savings.

The winter fuel allowance would be easier to deal with by involving the income tax system. Require it to be declared on your tax form, and tax it at 100%, much in the way that family allowance was clawed back years ago. But at what income level would you become "undeserving". Are there any politicians, not a notably courageous breed, would be prepared to introduce a 100% tax rate?

Mr Clegg's favourite wheeze is his wealth tax. This would involve imposing a tax on all assets, at a rate of 10% it is said, assets which will already have been taxed under the income tax system, or will be when you retire (your pension), and later when you die (death duty). Your assessed wealth will include, in addition to any savings and investments, the value of your home if you own it, and your pension fund. Consider the case a moderately successful teacher, say, or a civil servant or a police officer, earning £45,000 a year. Suppose such to be a homeowner living in a house worth £300,000. His or her expectation would be to retire (depending on length of service) on a two thirds pension of £30,000, which would be valued in "pension pot" terms at £600,000. The total "wealth" of such a person would therefore be £900,000, not far short of Cleggie's definition of the wealthy. If they were fortunate enough to have inherited a few quid or put a bit aside this notional wealth could reach a million, on which they would have to pay a tax of 10% which would wipe out their savings in the first year, or require them to sell up and move to a £200,000 house.

My worry, of course, is if they were to value pension funds after retirement, when the value would have to take into account life   expectancy. This presents the prospect of OAPs, immediately upon retirement, taking up smoking in order to reduce their likely longevity, and so devalue their "pension pots" actuarially speaking in order to avoid tax. Has Cleggie thought this through, I wonder?

I wouldn't like you to think that any of this is stopping me from enjoying retirement, though the pace is different. Before I retired I would, typically, toddle down to the Groucho Club, my Soho bolthole, where I would have a jolly good time surrounded by writers, television personalities, "personalities", and a sprinkling of wandering transvestites before going home at 1am. Last Friday, in contrast, I went to Yates's for their wine and nibbles preview of the autumn lines in their clothing department, and was home by eight thirty with a new winter coat. And not a transvestite in sight.

Beware contact with politicians

You may have noticed that the snapshot of me that has appeared over this column for eighteen months has been removed and another substituted. You may also, like me, have been surprised by this turn of events. This "improvement" was got up, behind my back, by Mrs Croft and my handler at the Mercury. Their thinking, if that is what was going in their heads, is that the older version made me look grumpy. Exactly; that is why I chose it. But, without so much as a kiss my bottom, they went ahead.

What is more, the substitute will bring back some bitter memories as it is the one I used in my election literature at the time of my ill-advised run in the District Council elections last year. You will remember that I was roundly seen off by the Big Beasts in the local political jungle, Councillors Andrews, Burr and Hopkinson. Those of you who voted for me will not welcome this reminder that you wasted your votes on a loser who didn't come up to snuff.

On the subject of politicians, I have come to the view that contact with them, which I always advise against, almost invariably leads to a mysterious neurological disorder the symptoms of which are nausea, failing eyesight followed by imbecility and, in the absence of medical intervention, an early death.

I have only ever met two big league politicians: Frank "Poor Old Dobbo" Dobson, who was cruelly forced by Tony Blair into a futile run against Livingstone for London Mayor, and Michael Portillo who pounced on me on Notting Hill Gate in an obsequious attempt to secure my vote. Poor Old Dobbo I ran into in a deli in Soho where he was demanding from the mystified Italians "a nice piece of mousetrap". Following these encounters I fell ill. I don't know how they do it – it's as if they exude organophosphates.

Anyway, last week I planned to devote my time to preparations for winter; supervising a delivery of logs to my store, getting the 'flu jab, choosing a new warm coat (at a keen price) for dog walking and fixing myself up with a new pair of hearing aids.

I was well embarked on these chores when I was struck down by two medical conditions. First was a gross sub-mandibular swelling, very painful, which I instantly diagnosed as sudden onset Derbyshire neck.

My physician did not support this diagnosis, proposing instead a possible stone in the duct. How, I wondered, had my kidney managed to migrate to my throat? Luckily my doctor is made of sterner stuff than most and doesn't insist that I make the decisions with him, decisions for which he has been prepared by many years of training, whereas I am guided only by night terrors. I always say, "If I were your father, what would you tell me to do?", and he always looks happy.

My second affliction was a nasty attack of winter vomiting disease, a particularly beastly virus that lays you very low, which sent me to my bed where my recuperation was disrupted by electricity failure in the house, which took half a day to sort out. It is from my bed of pain and misery that I rose to write to you today.

I particularly wanted to write about my disappointment when I saw the categories for the Pride of Malton and Norton awards.

There is no category into which I might fit. I am thinking there should be something along the lines of Most Promising Newspaper Columnist Pushing Seventy, for which you could once again have an opportunity to vote for me.

I doubt if the Pooh-Bahs who control these things would find such an innovation attractive. Perhaps because many of them are scribblers themselves? Or because they are over seventy, or look it at least?

A novel approach to planning

The Appeal decision, in respect of the proposed development of the Livestock Market site, has been received and Ryedale District Council's refusal to grant permission to the Fitzwilliam Estate has been overturned. The full report from the Planning Inspector runs to over twenty closely typed pages; it is not an easy read for those who, like me, are not familiar with planning laws and processes, or the details of the refusal itself.

Notwithstanding the guarded and courteous language used by the Planning Inspector, a clear and troubling picture emerges. The report is littered with such phrases as "the Council's position changed somewhat on certain points"; "Council Officers adopted what the Council referred to as a "novel" application of the sequential test"; "significant flaws in the way this matter had been approached (by the Council)"; "no firm evidence has been placed before me (by the Council)"; "the Council does not accept that the Livestock Market site forms a logical extension to the town centre, but this does not sit comfortably with its reason for refusal, which quite clearly states the contrary view"; "the Council has not submitted any firm evidence in what ways the proposal would be harmful"; "the Council has not undertaken any specific assessment"; "there is no adopted policy backing for the Council's stance"; "no firm, factual evidence has been placed before me".

And so it goes on. The whole sorry business as portrayed in the Inspector's report is characterised by staff work that can be described, generously, as mediocre (in one instance, by the Inspector, as inexcusable) and slapdash. One wonders to what extent, if any, Council Officers were under pressure to tailor their professional judgements in favour of the Council's known ambitions for its own assets. I do not know what would be better for them: to be seen to be incompetent, or to be suspected of having bent the knee of professional integrity.

What is not in doubt is that much damage has been done: to the Council's reputation for grasp of, and respect for process and regulation; to the finances of the Council, a price that will be paid by local householders; to the reputations of some Council employees, and possibly to their career prospects; and to the community in the consequential delay to much needed commercial development in the town.

Some, but not all, of this damage may be mitigated by the way in which the Council conducts itself in this situation, which it neither likes nor intended to come about. A good start would be to engage and co-operate in an even-handed way with the Fitzwilliam Estate to press forward with much needed change, and to resist the temptation to use its powers as the planning authority to frustrate, to delay and to seek retribution. A bit of staff training in planning law, process and ethics wouldn't come amiss either. Remediation, not retribution.

Having read the statement from the Leader of Ryedale District Council, Cllr Keith Knaggs, I am not hopeful – it is combative, not conciliatory. He puts the situation, which is not to his liking, down to "the difficulties which can arise from a single unelected individual sitting in judgement on the decisions of those elected by the public." Occupying a position by virtue of election is not a circumstance that precludes the possibilities of oversight and correction, and nor should it. Judges are not elected, not yet anyway, but they are in a position to give elected politicians a warm time if they act unlawfully, and to reverse their decisions. Not a rare eventuality.

Like most people I suppose, I don't much mind when the Council makes decisions I don't like or disagree with; it is to be expected, and it gives us something to rant about over a pint. What I do mind is the level of incompetence, and carelessness with process, that has been revealed by the Planning Inspector. During my career in the relatively gentlemanly world of academic publishing such a bravura display of ineptitude would have been followed by an unmistakeable sound – that of heads rolling.

A case of hypochondria

It has always been my practice, when medication is prescribed by my doctor, to discard unread the patient information leaflet that comes with the pills.

I do this not because I am cavalier when it comes to such matters, but for reasons of temperament. I know that if I read the lists of possible side effects I shall instantly detect in myself symptoms of all of them, even those that can only possibly afflict women. Side effects are roughly categorised as: "fairly common, but don't worry" (rashes, nausea), "rare" (night terrors, gastro-intestinal uproar, sudden blindness) and "so rare it's hardly worth mentioning, but we don't want to be sued" (exploding liver, catastrophic kidney failure, suicidal ideation, sudden death).

So comprehensive are these lists that they all pretty much resemble each other, irrespective of the medicine, and some warnings are quite ludicrous; for example, when taking sleep medication you will be solemnly warned about the possibility of drowsiness. It is the third category to which I am most susceptible.

For reasons of patient confidentiality and painful shyness, I cannot possibly go into great detail about my medical history, but here's a thing. A few years ago, when my blood cholesterol was found to be above normal, possibly because of my fondness for cheese and

Horlicks, I was prescribed a statin. This is a medication that miraculously lowers blood cholesterol, so miraculously that drug companies would like to put it in our drinking water (at our expense). A few months ago I collected my twenty-eight-day fix and promptly lost the lot. I decided that I could not confess this to my doctor, feeling guilty as I did about the cost implications (I too am a tax-payer), but instead thought the best bet would be to skip a month and keep mum. Something surprising happened.

After a couple of weeks, I noticed that my energy levels sky-rocketed and I was overwhelmed by a tremendous feeling of well-being. I felt ten years younger. Suddenly I found I wanted nothing more than to split logs, open my mail and deal with it, and replace light bulbs as soon as they blew. I stopped lying awake at night feeling my body for malignant lumps (and finding them, though by the morning they had cleared up), and a new optimism came over me. So I skipped the pills for another month, and then a third. But I had some concerns about deceiving my doctor, blissful in his belief that I was popping the pills regular.

At this point I was called for a routine blood test to monitor the level of my blood cholesterol. When the blood was drawn I expected to notice a layer of dripping on the surface of the sample, such as you see on a boat of cooling gravy, but it looked OK to me. A week later I bobbed in to the surgery to see if I had passed. I had, with flying colours – no further action required, I was told by Reception. But I felt that I should turn myself in to the doctor for wilful non-compliance, and throw myself on his mercy. Which I did.

I explained to him what had happened, adding that my family had noticed my decline into a near vegetativee state when I started popping the pills (which they failed to mention to me), and that they had also noticed my recent return from the legions of the living dead. He spotted at once that what I had described was by no means a double-blind crossover pharmaceutical trial, and that the patient sample was unusually small. "Connection does not prove cause", I could hear him thinking. But I didn't get the harsh scolding I had been expecting, and felt that I deserved, nor was I kicked off his list. Instead, he proposed a cunning plan.

The plan is that I shall stay off the meds for the time being, take another test in six months and if it shows an unacceptable elevation in blood cholesterol possibly go back on a statin, a different one perhaps. If, following this, I plunge back into miserable lassitude we'll discuss the next step.

This is medicine practised as William Osler would have liked to hear about. To have responded without irritation to the appearance during a busy clinic of a patient without a single symptom to report, indeed to report only a feeling of wellbeing, may be unusual (I don't know) but certainly it is welcome. I wonder what entry he made in my notes? "Inclined to meddle in his own medication", perhaps. Which would be fair enough, I suppose.

The moral of this story is – always read the patient information sheet. Unless you're a hypochondriac.

2013

Happier here than anywhere else

When, exhausted from years of living the metropolitan life, drinking cappuccino coffees and dodging the wandering transvestites on my way to the Groucho Club, I decided to retire to North, there were doubts expressed. Even my own son, Edward, was among the Doubting Thomases saying, in that lofty way of his, "I give it six months".

Now, after seven Christmases here, I feel confident publicly to review my situation. First, let me say that I am happier here than anywhere I have ever lived. It is often said that London is a collection of villages, but it is not true; transplant a family from, say Sinnington, into Notting Hill Gate and they would, even after a generation, confirm this.

So what's to like? A recent experience of mine will illustrate a part of it. I drove into the Derwent Practice car park where I left my Morris Minor, and reported to the nurses' station to make an appointment to have my ears syringed. That done, I shuffled round to the railway station to book a ticket to London for the following week when I would be attending an important meeting. When I got to the car, my keys were nowhere to be found. Having already forgotten that I had been to the railway station, I went to the nurses' reception to ask if I had left them on the counter. They were very concerned, did a search and, coming up empty handed, bent their minds to my problem. "Have you", one of them said, "been anywhere else?" I denied this possibility, but just as it looked as if the next question might be, "Can you tell me the name of the Prime Minister?" I remembered that I had.

Back to the railway station where I found the booking clerk, Dave, with the telephone directory in one hand, my car keys in the other, looking up my number so that he could ring me to let me know he had my keys. When, a few days later, I went in for the ear-thrutching, I was asked if I had found my keys. I have never lived in a place where such things were even remotely likely.

Recently, as I was patrolling about in Morrison's on the lookout for bargains, a lady approached me: "Excuse me. Do you mind if I ask you about your hearing aids?" It turned out that she had been trying to get her husband to get fixed up with some but had been meeting some resistance, and she was interested in getting some first hand feedback on the pros and cons from an obviously seasoned user. We had a pleasant chat during which I assumed an expression of what I hoped was one of accommodating niceness and described my experiences; she seemed happy enough, and off we both darted along the aisles to continue our evaluation of the specials. It seemed a perfectly natural episode at the time but I later reflected that had I received such an approach on a London Street my immediate reaction would have been: This is a lunatic. But not here, and it obviously didn't occur to her that this is how she might be viewed.

In London other drivers seldom give way to you, and if you give way to them they seldom give any acknowledgement. Here, I am frequently let in, or out – but, and Mrs Croft will bear me out in this, it is usually men who supply such courtesies, and give a nod or wave to indicate thanks. In the supermarket, on the other hand, in a congestion of trolleys situation it is the other way round. Women are co-operative and thoughtful, but men won't even catch your eye. I don't know why this is – is it, I wonder, that men pushing trolleys feel that they are in some way engaged in an unmanly activity?

But there it is – I wouldn't go back to what I had before, not even on the end of a barge pole. Even my son has been asking about the price of property up here. I think if Betty's set up shop here in Malton he'd be up here in a shot.

Eventful start to the grim hiatus

The grim hiatus between Christmas and St Valentine's Day (always a big event at our house) got off to an interesting start. Early in January while walking Rosie on our usual route I noticed that two horses and a foal had escaped from their paddock. They were exercising their freedom by galloping about on largely unfenced agricultural land. Not knowing the owner of these animals, or of the paddock, and given the proximity of the main road, I decided to report it to the police.

I legged it down to Malton police station, but it was closed (it was a Saturday), and the telephone hotline by the door was out of order. Luckily, I came upon a police traffic car, lurking in Town Street in the hope of catching uninsured drivers. The officer took all the details including, mysteriously, my date of birth – can I look forward to a birthday card in September? Anyway, that was that, and I thought no more about it.

Then blow me, a few days later, just as I was embarking on a pre-dinner bottle of Chardonnay with Mrs Croft, the door bell went and it turned out to be a police officer come to call - WPC Kay Londike. I assumed that she had come to thank me for my public spiritedness, but not a bit of it. She told me she was looking for a man whose name, although familiar to me, is not my own, and I noticed her hand hovering over her pepper spray, which made me anxious. I am not he, I told her grammatically, but I have already reported him to you. She was stunned.

I invited her in and explained that a person of the name she mentioned, whom she obviously thought she had tracked to my house, had been using my address for purposes that looked dodgy to me. I was able to provide her with vital clues, including his car registration number, which I am sure will facilitate more effective sleuthing leading to, possibly, accelerated promotion, and a position in the plain clothes branch. Unfortunately, I was unable to discover what would have been my fate had I turned out to be the blighter she was after; was I "wanted", a "person of interest", or had I merely driven off without paying after filling up the car? No amount of forensic probing on my part could get anything out of her – real secret service stuff.

More delights in the press (not the New Year Honours list – again). You may have noticed reports in the press over the years of blameless pensioners being asked to prove their age when trying to buy a bottle of wine in supermarkets, and mothers with toddlers on the same errand being turned away on the grounds that the booze "might" be intended for the children. Things have got stricter. A woman presented herself at a supermarket checkout with, among her groceries, a set of dessert spoons. She was refused the purchase because the spoons could be put to use as drug-taking paraphernalia, cooking heroin I suppose. Her sprouts were OK, she could cook those, but sprouts are good for you. Well, quite so. Equally, the spoons could have been intended for equipping a group of primitive music makers who would go on to give performances on premises not licensed to put spoons concerts. Just as well, then, that they were seized at the till.

You wonder where the supermarkets find these people with such lively imaginations, and inside knowledge of the techniques of preparing illegal substances for consumption. If you are tempted to buy a clothes line be careful to arrange your face into an expression of blithe innocence, lest you be suspected of equipping yourself with a garrotte intended for the disposal of a family member. And where do they find the spokesmen who respond when these incidents occur? On this occasion the response was that the spoons had been inadvertently miscoded on "the system", and showed up on the screen as steak knives, an unconvincing explanation. Did the check-out employee not look at what was in her hands, and in any case can't we buy sharp cutlery any more? How are we to deal with a tough chop? It is a strange world we live in.

I worry about those horses, especially the foal to whom I had become rather attached, and I wonder if the Mr Big, on the run from who knows what, has been firmly banged up.

John Foley – An officer and a gentleman

My late father-in-law, John Foley, was a citizen of Eire. After qualifying in medicine in Dublin he moved to England where he worked briefly, in what may have been a pre-registration post, as a general practitioner in Hull of all places. At 723 Beverley High Road, to be exact, an address that houses a family medical practice to this day, more than 70 years later. He died in 1972.

In 1941 he enlisted in the Royal Navy Reserve (RNVR), saw active service throughout the Second World War and was discharged in 1946 in the rank of Surgeon Lieutenant Commander. As a result of a dramatic episode during his naval career, involving a young German submariner, of which more later, some research by his children turned up, among other things, his personal file, released by the Royal Navy. The file consists largely of personal assessments made by his various commanding officers; these are revealing.

These assessments take the form of scores out of ten for five personal characteristics: Professional Ability, Personal Qualities, Leadership, Intellectual Ability and Administrative Ability. There is also provision for free text expression of opinion.

Given that the eight assessments were made by eight different officers, some of whom will "mark" more or less generously than others, you would expect some variation. Also, it is a very subjective process, particularly judging intellectual ability, for example; it is not uncommon for the garrulous (or the taciturn) to be judged, on the basis of their prolixity (or reticence), to be bright. Or stupid. You might also expect a naval captain to better equipped, by experience and better informed in the matter of assessing qualities of leadership and administrative skills, say, than surgical ability. In fact, the total scores given of all categories are in the range 32 (out of 50) to 37, with an average of 35. This shows a high level of consistency. But, only if you exclude one particular officer's effort.

In his case the total marks given was ten, with his surgical/medical rating being only one (all other officers scored 7 or eight), and his intelligence plunged, for one six-month period only, by fifty percent.

My brother-in-law claims that astonishing outlier is explained entirely by the fact that this officer's name was Rupert. This is not a scientific explanation, but it has a seductive simplicity.

The various comments are interesting. "A typical Irishman", says one, "inclined to be a bit wild at first, but has now settled down. Has the full confidence of the officers and ship's company. Very good at rugger." Another: "A thoroughly good type of officer with a sound service outlook.....considerable charm and mixes well in the mess." A third: "An excellent officer.......his service attitude is excellent. If he should ever seek transference to RN (from RNVR) I should select him without hesitation. Exceptionally outstanding." And it goes on: "A likeable and sensible Irishman; has a good manner with men. Will act very quickly when required."

What does Rupert have to say? "This officer may have a talent for his profession (but he scored him only one out of ten anyway) but after repeated warnings will not behave himself like an officer and a gentleman. He is idle, unreliable and critical and seems unable to adapt himself to the routine of ship life. He is frequently the worse for liquor both on board and on shore. I have frequently had occasion to admonish this officer for unseemly conduct due to drink." Considering John Foley had at least two ships sunk under him (and he wouldn't have been driving), it is hardly surprising that he took solace in a few nips. Anyway, that's Rupert for you. Sadly his surname was not Queeg.

It is clear from these reports that John Foley was well-liked by officers and men and that his medical skills ("very painstaking and zealous in matters concerning the health of the ship's company" is a typical comment), but Rupert wasn't happy. Didn't like Irishmen, perhaps.

A picture of colonial life

In the seventies I was bundled off by my employer, an educational publishing company, to what was then Rhodesia (now Zimbabwe) where I would be a key player in preparing the local company for the anticipated "settlement" with Ian Smith. Rhodesia was then a rebel colony, having declared unilateral independence from Britain in an attempt to stave off majority (black) rule and Harold Wilson was on the case, holding secret talks on board Royal Navy ships in search of a solution. Not so secret, however, that the tabloid newspapers didn't know all about it.

And so it was that I encountered a strange character called Ben Gingell. Ben had gone from the UK as a young man, just like me, for a tour of duty, but unlike me he loved it so much he never came back, staying to establish an eccentric lifestyle. Shortly after my arrival, which had been dreading, he invited to a dinner at his home, a fine house called Jericho Lodge. His guests assembled in a comfortable room where we drank large gin and tonics, a popular drink liberally taken in the belief that the quinine in the tonic prevented malaria. Perhaps it did; it certainly promoted yellow complexions and liver disease (the gin, possibly), both conditions commonly found among the old colonial hands.

After several vases of gin apiece, the double doors to the dining room burst open and in stepped Ben's manservant, Wil-son (emphasis on the second syllable). He was dressed in a white jacket and trousers, with a scarlet cummerbund and a diagonal sash, topped off with a jaunty fez, also scarlet. He carried a shiny bugle, on which he gave three sharp toots, and bawled "Master! Dinner is served!" And in we all trooped. Wil-son efficiently served up the food he had skilfully prepared, and Ben kept our wine glasses full with words of encouragement: "Howard, my boy! A drop more wine to steady you".

At the end of the meal Ben's lady, a widow who would later become his wife, led the women out to powder their noses and Ben distributed cigars and brandy to the men. With all the men fixed up, Ben opened the French windows onto the garden saying, "Gentlemen, step aside into Africa I beg of you", which we did. Being the new boy, I hung back a bit to see what this was all about; my fellow guests, more familiar with Ben's hospitality, immediately set about urinating on the lawn. We were also being given an opportunity to powder our noses. I later discovered that "stepping aside" was Ben's euphemism for visiting the loo, and I still find myself occasionally using it more than thirty years later.

We rejoined the ladies in the withdrawing room for some serious postprandial boozing, and after while Wil-son came in again, gave a few toots on his bugle and introduced his doxy, known in Scotland as a bidie-in. This was Weezy-weezy. They both bowed deeply to each of us in turn, wishing us goodnight, and as they retreated (backwards) into the kitchen, Ben called out, "Wil-son, my boy! Take a bottle of beer from the fridge, I beg of you!"

This was a picture of colonial life that was already history throughout the continent, apart from in Southern Africa where it lingered on, but not for much longer. I was fortunate personally to witness through this vignette, and others like it, a slice of life that had largely disappeared. And I was fortunate to meet, and briefly to get to know a man whose odd life had turned him into an eccentric who I thought would be unlikely to survive either in the new Zimbabwe, or back in Britain. And so it turned out. The political settlement, the expectation of which propelled me to that strange place, did not materialise until many years later and when it did Ben was repatriated to England where, after a few months and at a relatively young age, he died.

I noticed that Ben, who always addressed me as "my boy", as soon as he knew that I was being recalled upgraded me to "my dear boy", even, after a few drinks, "my shining boy". I'm glad I knew him. He was more pleased to see the back of me, when I was posted on to Nigeria, than anyone I have known, and that's saying something. May light perpetual shine upon him.

Footnote: With Ben's euphemism for tapping the bladder never far from my thoughts, I was greatly entertained by reports of senior BBC managers "stepping aside" during the early stages of the Jimmy Savile fiasco. In this case a euphemism for, I suppose, running for cover, though loss of bladder control may also have been involved.

Howard Croft? Been dead for years

While it is often observed that people in the supermarket queue resent others eyeing up their purchases laid out on the belt, out of shyness perhaps about the large quantities of alcohol and fat-laden treats on show, they show no concern about their conversations being overheard. Many times I have picked up useful information about gynaecological difficulties when waiting to get to the till. Last week I heard a customer in the line asking another why she was buying so much Actimel, a yoghurt-like substance supplied in bottles small enough to imply medicinal properties.

The Actimel aficionado replied that it is excellent for promoting stability in cases of disorderly gastrointestinal functions and, getting to the science of it, explained that it encourages "friendly flora and fauna in the gut". Fauna? What happens do you suppose? Do badgers and field voles move in and set up home there, to raise families perhaps? This reminds me of a former colleague, a sharp faced fellow with a bushy beard. When his wife to be first introduced him to future father-in-law, an irascible retired colonel (you know the type, I'm sure), his first words were "Hah! Fella looks like a ferret peering out of a bear's backside". How did he know? Perhaps during his many military campaigns, he had served in a country where yoghurt is commonly fed to bears.

On the subject of supermarkets, the horsemeat in your burger scandal is shaping up pretty much like the BSE/mad cow disease of twenty odd years ago; early, bland assurances from politicians who minimised the problem, followed by mounting concerns, followed by alarmist predictions. The hunt for scapegoats is on, with government leading the charge in all directions other than at itself in the shape of the Food Standards Agency (FSA). Instead of the proactive analysis conducted by their Irish counterparts, who first spotted the horse-meat problem, they have allowed themselves to become distracted by the healthy eating and moderate drinking bandwagons. This found its most ludicrous expression in the FSA's campaign to persuade football fans to drink fizzy water with a squeeze of lemon in it when watching World Cup matches on the telly in pubs. What planet are these people on? Anyway, the obviously have more of an appetite for public education (not their brief) than for boring old public health, their main brief. No doubt in due course they'll find a way of blaming the farmers.

Although I accept that food labels should be true and wholly true, I was a bit surprised to read that Waitrose's meatballs have been found to be "tainted" with pork – 30% "tainted", in fact. Had I known that I might have bought some; or tried to anyway. I don't think I'm welcome there since I used my dog whistle to summon (successfully) Mrs Croft when she had wandered off. My favourite recipe for meat-balls (my daughter's) is 70% beef 30% pork, tainted also with onions. My other reason for steering clear of Waitrose, apart from being banned for life, is a crippling lack of class confidence. Fletcher's for me, where they don't turn their noses up if you shop in your wellies.

Speaking of unusually located ferrets, I was at a memorial service in London last week, attended by scores of former colleagues whom I had not seen for over thirty years, with all the attendant recognition problems of occasions. The first person I instantly recognised was the ferret, but now of the arctic variety – more a Cap'n Birdseye, in fact, but the pinched features unmistakable. From there it was all downhill all the way. A strange woman, elderly I would say, came up to me and asked, "I wonder if you can help me? Do you happen to know if Howard Croft is here?" It was a difficult question, and the honest answer not only would have involved embarrassing the poor woman, but would also have led to a conversation with someone whose earnest manner suggested a very dull time indeed. My reply? "Good heavens, no, he's been dead for years." And off I toddled in search of a more rewarding prospect. I later noticed her heading my way with a funny look on her face. I legged it to King's Cross. This reply, which I can only put down to panic, was later described as "a grave social error".

Note: Following my treatise on the state of the world shortage of flageolet beans, a kind reader (thank you, Enid) left a supply on my doorstep, which prompts me to mention that I am having difficulties in locating supplies of Krug champagne.

Decision makers need to step back and think

I have been reading about a nineteenth century politician called, ludicrously, Colonel Charles de Laet Waldo Sibthorp, described by the Dictionary of National Biography as "the embodiment of old fashioned prejudice". In addition to holding eccentric views, at the young age of 43 he dressed in a style that had gone out of fashion long before he was born and he invariably carried on a chain round his neck a quizzing glass, also no longer modish.

He was hostile to change in all its forms, perhaps because he was surrounded by it. At the same time as reading about Sibthorp I was wrestling with the arguments about the proposed HS2 rail route from London to Manchester and Leeds that will dramatically reduce journey times. In the case of Leeds I can just about understand it, but why anyone might consider reaching Manchester more quickly an advantage is beyond me.

I wonder what Sibthorp would have made of it all? He was particularly exercised by the introduction of railways in the 19th Century, referring to them as "dangerous novelties". It is true that the Government has invoked the Victorian push for progress in which the benefits envisaged would be enjoyed not by proponents of innovation but by future generations, implausible though the predictions of the fruits of HS2 are. Sibthorp, I imagine would be appalled.

The Victorian innovators were, of course, motivated by a desire to become rich but there was too, mixed in with that, a rather virtuous concern to leave a mark by improving life "going forward". We continue to enjoy the public health and engineering achievements of that time while, typically, shamefully neglecting them.

But it seems to me to be different now. Rather than selflessly disregarding the fact that they personally will not benefit from the progress they are fighting for, I suspect that our politicians and their advisers comfort themselves with the knowledge that, when it all goes wrong, they will be long gone. We see this, too, at a local level. We have seen, yet again, several heavy duty water pumps working overtime in Old Malton diverting surface water into the Derwent to prevent flooding. And yet, only half a mile away, the geniuses in Ryedale House are preparing to give long term approval to the development of over a hundred hectares of land north of the A64 bypass. This will involve, perhaps, two thousand houses and goodness knows what else, with a sharp reduction in the local capacity to absorb rain and snow melt.

However, the consequences (more and worse flooding) will only hit us when the current crop of councillors and their supine officials are safely tucked up in caring institutions, being fed through straws and fiddling absently with the Velcro fasteners on their slippers. Then they won't give a toss, but we can make them do so now. The focus of the problem is in Old Malton, but it will impact on both Malton and Norton, and we should all vociferously oppose this short term, borderline lunacy. Remember, these are the people who led us into the immensely costly Wentworth Street fiasco. Like the Bourbons, they have forgotten nothing and learnt nothing. I'm not referring to biscuits here; but cream crackers would fit.

The mention of borderline lunacy brings me back to good old Sibthorp. He shared the Duke of Wellington's reason for opposing the railways, that "they encourage the working classes to move about". He was fiercely opposed to the new fangled water closets, largely unchanged to this day, preferring the old system, too disgusting to describe. He, although odd, and for the wrong reasons, would support us

In one vital matter he was foresighted. He predicted that the powers of the new sanitary inspectors would entitle them to enter the house of the lord mayor of York to discover what he had for dinner, and whether he went to bed sober. He was right; I read recently that council officials have over two hundred legitimate grounds forcibly to enter our homes and sniff about.

Finally, he denounced the Great Exhibition of 1851 on the grounds that it would attract large numbers of foreigners and criminals, and advised "persons living near Hyde Park to keep a sharp look-out for their silver cutlery and servant maids". Exactly my concerns when I heard the Olympics were coming to town. What?

Thinking caps on for my Book Festival quiz

You may remember that during last year's Ryedale literary Festival a bookish quiz was held in the Milton Rooms, Malton. What you may have forgotten is that Team Taylor-Croft, with a tsunami of esoteric erudition, swept the board and carried off the trophies. This year, as part of World Book Day, another quiz is to be held, this time in Pickering, and to prevent the possibility, some would say certainty, of another humiliating rout by Team Taylor-Croft last year's victors have been commissioned to compile the questions.

Michael and Susie Taylor, Mrs Croft and myself were too ready for such a purpose, and the result is a mixed challenge. Rigorous intellectual testing in some sections (mine) will require knowledge of, say, Wordsworth's inside leg measurements and Goethe's hat size, will contrast sharply with more rudimentary demands in others (Mrs Croft's) where knowing what Milly Molly Mandy did next will score easy points. Something for everyone, I think.

In addition to all this excitement I shall myself be putting in a personal appearance, an event that will not match for news value that day, a few years ago, when the presumed-dead Elvis went into a supermarket in Colchester to buy a tin of sardines. But that's Pickering for you.

The quiz will be held at the Sun Inn on Westgate, Pickering, in their newly refurbished conservatory, at 7.30pm on Tuesday the 23rd of April, admission £10 per team (maximum four); tickets will be on sale at the door. Capacity is limited to 44.

Close students of this column will remember reading about my ganglion, expertly diagnosed by my physician. A number of readers have been kind enough to stop me in the street to show me their own ganglia, adding greatly to my already impressive fund of clinical knowledge. Derek Fox, raconteur, butcher, purveyor of game and sometime Retail Personality of the Year, provided details of his own medical history ganglion-wise. It seems that when he was afflicted no family Bible could be found to flatten the blighter so he bashed it instead with his sister's prayer book, to such good effect that the following morning the growth had vanished. Mrs Fox, on the other hand, was able to show me her currently active ganglion; I assume that the prayer book has by now gone the way of the family Bible. I am not – you may be surprised to hear this – medically qualified, but I did feel confident enough to prescribe a good whacking with a frozen leg of spring lamb. I am confident that no further consultations will be required.

On the subject unqualified medical experts, I see that Councillor Linda Cowling, having taken over, from Councillor Knaggs, the reins of the now minority Conservative Party, is demonstrating wisdom and expertise in the areas of obesity and social isolation. Speaking about her new strategy to support and improve sporting provision, which is the result of months of research, consultation and deliberation "right across Ryedale", she revealed the outcome: there will be "green gyms", "trim trails", and the Indoor Bowls Club will be closed. A trim trail is a new one on me, and I look forward to learning more. Are they, I wonder, something along the lines of pub crawls but instead of touring pubs and drinking yourself into a coma you call in at several barber shops and get your hair cut? Not much in that for baldies such as me.

Worryingly, Councillor Cowling has upgraded the obesity alert from epidemic to pandemic, a disturbing development of which the Royal College of Physicians seems to be unaware. Perhaps she has Eric Pickles in mind. But I bow to her greater insights into social isolation. It is an affliction commonly suffered by Conservatives – I have been accused of many things in my time, but never of being one of those.

I look forward to greeting you all at the Sun Inn on the 23rd April. Following an unfortunate attempt at cheating last year, once the game is on visits to the WCs will be forbidden (if in doubt get yourself catheterised for the evening), and mobile 'phones will be confiscated on sight and destroyed. As Elvis would say, be there or be square.

Heated seats, great for warming fish suppers

Having stooped to fill the dog's bowl, and running late, I rose and turned in a single, swift movement familiar to fans of the great Nijinsky. I am talking ballet here, not horse racing. Not being as lithe as once I was, I put my back out, which I don't suppose Nijinsky ever did. The reason for my haste was that I was about to drive 320 miles to Chichester, not the best plan with a dodgy back.

Luckily, my car has heated seats that not only warm up the bottom but also the lumbar region – just the ticket for supplying healing warmth to a sprained back, I thought. I have never before used this facility when driving, though I have used it on the passenger side when transporting fish suppers from the chippie to keep them in peak condition. A useful tip this. So off I set, driving like Jehu and receiving therapy at the same time. When I reached Doncaster, and sweating a bit, I remembered my mother's advice never to sit on radiators because, as she put it, "you'll catch piles".

Mothers in my experience are very interested in piles, and mine certainly regarded herself as a bit of an expert, but why she set herself up as an expert on radiators I can't think; we had none in the home, and I don't suppose I ever mentioned having them in the classrooms at school. Anyway, the advice had stuck, and here I was, caught between the rock of haemorrhoids and the hard place of low back pain, near Doncaster with nearly three hundred miles to go. I switched off the heat and arrived in Chichester doubled over with pain and moving only with great difficulty – more Quasimodo than

Nijinsky - but otherwise at ease.

The stay in Chichester was not without incident. I attempt to mend a puncture on mother-in-law's wheelchair, with a dismal want of success, in part because the bicycle pump I had bought was, because cheap, useless. Mrs Croft, with an air of resentment I thought quite uncalled for, threw the wheelchair into the back of the car and took it to Halford's where "a nice young man" fixed things (not a puncture, as it turned out) in a jiffy for no charge and sold her a high end pump for quite a price and proved that large companies can provide personal service. Not that this does much to ease marital tension.

Another highlight of our visit was handing over mother-in-law's Grand National winnings, substantial winnings I may say, which came from a shrewd bet I had placed on her behalf on a nag of her choosing. At 66/1 no less. This was immediately blown on a new telly, bought on Friday, delivered and installed on Saturday. Unfortunately, when the installer arrived I was "home alone", due to heavy shopping demands on the ladies, with a packet of biscuits and low self-esteem following poor performance on the puncture outfit front, and little confidence that I would be able adequately to supervise matters. All went well, however, and the telly, which speaks to you when you make adjustments, a feature that may take some getting used to, works well and my biscuits were not, as I had feared, confiscated. Indeed, I was presented with two fine new shirts, one from each of them, and a chocolate éclair, and I quickly forgot how shabbily I had been treated earlier over my flat tyre failure.

More good news on the Masterchef front. My friend Saira swept effortlessly into the next phase of the challenge after cooking something she described as "Bangladeshi street food", whatever that means. It did the trick, though. She used to claim to be Welsh, having been born in Cardiff, which I suppose is fair enough, but being born in a stable doesn't make you a horse, and her Mum and Dad came from Bangladesh. I don't mind either way, and the shift in identity avoided the temptation to do salt marsh lamb and laverbread. She's looking good, I must say, and the Talbot Hotel, Malton is "following her on Twitter", which may be significant. Or not.

Bores and socks with sandals have no place!

As our doughty District Council battles on through the summer in its unenviable task of governing the ungovernable, it will be cheered by new powers, announced in the Queen's Speech, giving them the right to create new crimes, more or less willy nilly, and therefore limitless opportunities for bossiness.

Councils will be able to issue Public Space Protection Orders (PSPOs) making it a crime to do anything they, the councils, doesn't fancy. The intention of this poorly defined power is to curb nuisance behaviour, which sounds OK, but it is up to councils to define what constitutes a nuisance, and gives the green light to over-zealous council officials to mount their personal hobby horses in ways not intended. Councils' readiness to abuse powers given to them under anti-terrorism legislation (RIPA) may guide us here; covert surveillance conducted on the public, and indeed on their own staff, in respect of trivial matters with a casual ease much envied by police officers concerned with graver problems, and burdened by stretched resources.

No sensible person would argue with the need to deal with drunkards and uncontrolled dogs in public places, already covered by existing law, but it could go much further. If, for example, I should choose to relax outside my front door with a glass of claret and, enjoying a cigar, watch speeding motorists, a popular feature round our way, it would be perfectly lawful for a passing council officer to declare it a crime; the cigar, the wine, or just hanging about on the pavement. Mulish persistence on my part would lead to prosecution in the criminal courts.

If I were a council officer with such powers delegated to me I would systematically set about eradicating behaviour that displeases me. I once was a member of a club under whose rules membership could be withdrawn on only two grounds: wearing socks with sandals, and persistently introducing boring guests. This would be a good start. I would criminalise bores. I am not aware of bores congregating in the street, though they may, not being identifiable simply by visual inspection, so sly manoeuvres might be necessary. If for example I were to be invited to a dinner party only to find myself surrounded by bores I could suggest to my host that we step out front with our glasses of wine, along with the boring guests with their shandies, to watch the speeding motorists. Then I would pounce. We would be in a public place.

Matters of dress are easier. Socks and sandals would definitely be out. Only those with a note from the doctor, to be carried at all times along the lines of the old South African pass laws, would be permitted in public spaces dressed in this way. Similarly, no male cyclist over the age of forty would be allowed to go about in figure-hugging Lycra, though they would be permitted to dress like this in the privacy of their own homes and even to invite round a few like-minded friends similarly dressed. We don't want a police state after all. There would be warnings, of course, but not for men over the age of sixty wearing Lycra tighties; they would be liable to arrest on sight, and marched off to the bridewell.

You may think that this approach allows too much personal prejudice to creep in, but it happens already. In a recent documentary television programme about the work of planning officers we saw one such individual dismiss out of hand a proposal with the words "it looks weird". She may have said other things off-camera, of course, but presumably this was her best shot. Personally, I agreed with her, but I also thought that she looked a bit weird. I hesitate to suggest that she be dismissed, but she should certainly be forbidden to go about in a conservation area except after dark. Not in keeping, as she doubtless would put it.

In the meantime, our own district council, eager to be seen to be doing something novel, has given the "youth" portfolio to a woman of 84, and made its "champion of the elderly" a young man, obviously keen, who is barely out of short trousers. Brilliant!

Presumably the "Wrinklie" Tsar has a granny, and the "Kiddie" Tsar has grandchildren, or knows someone who has, in which case they are ideally qualified to discharge their new responsibilities. I look forward to hearing what exciting initiatives they come up with.

Royal provenance and a thrifty way of life

This Totally Locally "hidden gems" business, of which you may be aware, seems to be going well, but it is producing some unlooked for side effects if what's going on in our house is anything to go by. A certain light-headedness in Mrs Croft for example. Fired up by promises of "five quid specials" on offer in every hidden gem shop she hobbled into Malton to snap up a few bargains. Nothing wrong with that, you may think.

But it didn't turn out quite as I had imagined. In Woodall's, for example, the "special" was a yard brush, only a fiver, but what she came out with was a superior item costing nearly twenty. The proprietor of Woodall's, with his amusing and convincing line in sales talk, persuaded her that this more costly top of the range article was a better buy on the grounds that it had been used personally by Her Majesty the Queen. Although I have met Her Majesty on a number of occasions I cannot claim anything approaching personal friendship, but I must say I didn't detect any signs – clawed hands, for example, or spinal curvature – that she spends much time sweeping up. I decided to investigate the authenticity of this claim.

When I arrived at Woodall's I was given a modified version of Mrs

Croft's implausible report. The Queen, I was told, had not actually swept up with this brush but merely held it to demonstrate the best angle of approach for optimum effectiveness before handing it over to a footman. The mere fact that HMQ had touched this implement had, on the same principal as touching for scrofula perhaps, enhanced its utility and likely durability. So I was told. As I was pondering the possibility of there being anything at all in this yarn, blow me down if said proprietor didn't offer me a strange looking multi-purpose knife, possibly illegal, that had been specially made for King George VI and personally used by him to peel fruit and spear prawns on the Royal barbecue. Plainly made from the finest steel with a hart's horn handle, and undeniable royal provenance, it was irresistible and I bought it on the spot. I shall use it to carve Mrs Croft's name on the handle of the broom as a reminder that this year it will be, finally, her turn to deal with the autumn leaves, dodgy knee or not.

Mrs Croft's enthusiasm for a five quid bargain chimes in with other surprising changes I have noticed lately. She has always been a bit of a spender. You may be aware of this; indeed, I may have mentioned it before. I, on the other hand, am more on the frugal side, careful if you like or, as she would say – frequently says – tight-fisted. But recently she has been representing herself as a model of thrift, turning off the garage lights several times a day even when I am in there operating my circular saw, which I admit allows for a more sinister interpretation than mere polishing of thrifty credentials. This is the woman who routinely fills the kettle and switches it on before going to bed at night, and invariably buys two green peppers when the recipe calls for only one. What is going on?

I do wonder if I am witnessing the onset of age related dottiness, but if so I think it hardly fair; she is considerably younger than me so surely it's my turn first. I discussed this with my daughter, who is constantly on the lookout for parental deterioration. I thought I might have unsettled her during a telephone call in which she asked me what the following week held in store for me. Embarrassed that the truthful answer was "not much" I strayed into cataloguing the events of the following week to make myself sound more interesting; was she concerned that I had confused two weeks? I called her back to reassure her, but she had, she said, no concerns along those lines. No, but what if, I asked, she were to hear reports that I had been found by the police strolling up Stonegate in York having forgotten that day to put on my trousers. Would she then be concerned? Not a bit, she replied, I would just assume you were pulling a stunt to get attention.

Charming young host welcomes an 'outsider'

I have lived in Old Malton for only a brief time (seven years), so brief a time that I occasionally find myself addressed as an "outsider". Well-informed locals assure me that if I stick it out for another 23 years, an unlikely eventuality given my age and the decades of punishment to which I have subjected my body, I might be promoted to "newcomer", a friendlier appellation. However, being a quick learner, I can now spot a typical Old Malton function and it was at one such that Mrs Croft and I found ourselves on Saturday.

It was an alfresco fund-raising dinner put on by a young neighbour, Holli Fletcher, who has discovered an urgent desire to spend some time in Borneo helping the locals with their much needed community projects. For this she needs money. She has already made considerable progress by various enterprises, some of them quite ingenious. The idea of this alfresco stunt was that a four course dinner would be provided to those who booked in, over 20 of us, and then at the end of the evening we would all discreetly slip into an envelope an amount of money corresponding to how good a time we had enjoyed.

It was clear to me that everyone had a rollicking good time. The food was excellent, the service was charming, and the menu choices mind boggling. I took along a bottle of my favourite Shiraz, thinking that a warming red would be welcome if the evening grew cooler, as they will do when the days grow shorter. I handed it over on arrival and when it was later brought to our table it was clear that, for some inexplicable reason, it had been kept in an ice bucket. It arrived-chilled to perfection, and to my surprise it drank very well. Holli knows her wine, evidently.

Holli, who was an enchanting host and made a more than competent speech at the end of the dinner outlining her plans, was tirelessly supported by her younger sister, Anais, on the waitressing front, with Mum and Dad on the logistical side lurking in the background. But what surprised us all was the appearance of a young conjurer. Holli is a Year 10 pupil at Malton School, a fourth former as we used to say, and the magician is school friend Matthew Woollons. He visited each of the tables to entertain us. I expected a few cheesy tricks from a tongue tied and ill at ease youth, but what we got was a revelation. With extraordinary deftness and confidence, accompanied by an amusing patter, he foxed us all.

It was a professional performance, and it came as no surprise to learn that he is a member of the Magic Circle. I am not as a rule much struck on this kind of entertainment, but it greatly enhanced the evening for us all and I look forward to seeing this performer again. I have not enjoyed such a bag of tricks since a professional magician, a flamboyant itinerant transvestite called, amusingly, Fay Presto interrupted my dinner in a smart London restaurant many years ago. My only criticism is that when challenged to pull a pigeon out of his bottom Matthew didn't even attempt it.

I am not entirely clear what Holli is going to do in Borneo. Re-point deteriorating brickwork perhaps, lay tarmac through the jungle or do a bit of elementary bone-setting. In an earlier, less enlightened age we would have expressed concern that she might be falling into the hands of head-shrinkers, but now the concerns are merely about malaria, yellow fever and cholera, all easily prevented. If I tell you that Holli raised over 800 quid that night you will be amazed, and I may be charged with multiple violations of the Data Protection Act and accused of undermining her right to privacy and family life as defined by the European Court of Human Rights. So keep it to yourselves.

I'm not sure if you can progress your status beyond "outsider" and "newcomer" in Old Malton, and if so to what (certainly not to "peaker"), but I am pretty sure I don't have enough years left to find out. In any case, I have only a 100 year lease on my grave in Old Malton Cemetery at which point presumably my bones will be dug up and thrown onto the by-pass by zealous council workers anxious to resell the plot, and I shall be past caring.

Neighbourhood Watch no substitute for carers

When I was a young man two groups of people stood higher than others in terms of respect in society: nurses and OAPs. Nurses, often referred to as "angels" in the tabloid press, enjoyed the support of industrial trade unionists, especially when they were being denied decent pay rises by heartless politicians. Miners, steelworkers and the like would from time to time offer to take strike action on their behalf.

Similarly, OAPs were seen as defenceless people who spent much of their time rinsing their NHS teeth under the cold tap, shivering in the winter and frequently the recipients of small acts of kindness from neighbours. Rosy cheeked housewives would pop round with occasional pies and puddings and offers of help with the rinsing.

There was even a touching episode in the seventies, when sugar workers were threatening to strike; assurances were given that during the strike emergency supplies of sugar would be made available for OAPs.

This has all changed. I have myself been an OAP for several years, but not once has a rosy cheeked housewife popped round to my place with enticing offerings; not a pie in sight, no buckets of coal discreetly left on my doorstep. Something has gone wrong. I blame the civil servants, no longer civil and only self-serving, with their stupendous pensions, which have by association rendered all OAPs the objects of loathing and envy. This has not been helped by press reports of even disgraced public sector workers slinking off into obscurity with "million pound pensions". Any mention now that one has a pension at all draws looks that you might reasonably expect if you had admitted to robbing a post office. Suggestions from government ministers that we voluntarily surrender our bus passes seem to be increasingly popular among the envious young.

As for nurses, one hears horror stories every day; of difficult patients being ruthlessly shunted onto the Liverpool Clinical Pathway. When first devised and introduced it sounded like a dream-like and kindly process of "easing the passing" of the terminally ill, as it probably was in the hands of its originators. But, having been "rolled out nationally" by the Department of Health in its wisdom, it rapidly came to resemble not a clinical pathway but the Burma Railway. It has become a tick-box process implemented by uncomprehending on the defenceless that few have survived. These lucky few, whose fearless relatives smuggled in water to sustain them, have in many cases rallied to such an extent that they have been able to return to normal life.

The Department of Health, in its new wisdom, has recommended that the Liverpool Pathway be used no longer. Just as the furious screams of prison guards have been silenced, no more shall we hear the abusive yelling of nurses who suspect that fluids, often disguised as vases of flowers, are being smuggled onto the wards to relieve patients' misery.

However, never to be found without a headline-grabbing initiative, the Department of Health has come up with another winner. The elderly and frail in our communities who need help with feeding and washing will henceforward become the responsibility of Neighbour-hood Watch teams.

These worthy, public spirited individuals who monitor our streets by looking out for shady looking characters and lie in wait for possible arsonists will in addition do duty spooning apple puree into those too feeble to feed themselves. And wash them.

I do not know any Neighbourhood Watch personnel, but I imagine that they are largely made up of retired police officers, off-duty firemen and tough looking former Queen's Scouts, with a few stern librarians thrown in to levy fines if necessary. I don't know about you, but I'm not sure that these are the people I want popping round to wash my bottom when I'm on my last knockings, much though we are in their debt for vigilance in other areas. My preference would be for well-trained (and probably re-trained) nurses. But not to worry; this will fall under the authority of local government for registration and implementation. It will never happen.

Left beached while others head for the beach

We are now into the time of the year I least like – August. The humidity, the electric storms, chums jetting off to places like Cyprus and the Netherland Antilles, some in search of melanomas, others to open or to close bank accounts. It is a dull time for those of us left behind. I have never been keen to develop a tan, a boring process of lying still for hours in an expensive location, and my most exotically placed bank account is somewhere in south London. I am one of the dull people left beached in the dullest month of the year while the glitterati flit about making adjustments to their exciting lives and toning their pale bodies in readiness for the winter.

Overlying this, there is the perennial worry about examination results. I have calculated that I have, over the last forty years, suffered this anxiety in over thirty of them. Thankfully, I see little prospect of even mild interest in coming years.

By the time my first grandchild is doing his "O" Levels I shall be, if spared, pushing eighty and, as my preoccupation with self-interest gathers speed, too busy thinking about myself to pay much attention. This concern about examination results is very scarring; although graduated almost fifty years ago, I still occasionally have that dream where I scan the posted degree results for my name and find it nowhere.

This year has been made more tiresome by a loose manhole cover in the road outside my house which makes a loud clanking noise wherever a Pickering bound vehicle passes over it. We called these "fever drains" when I was a child, or our parents did to keep us away from them, and out of the traffic. We liked to poke bamboo canes through the holes to see what we could come up with.

After several nights of interrupted sleep, complaining house guests and the wailing of distressed babies and dogs we reported this nuisance to Yorkshire Water. They referred us to their sub-contractor. A fellow with a clipboard and a liking for tea and biscuits quickly appeared to do a survey; with an air of authority he issued a "seven-day notice" and gave us an undertaking that the matter would be dealt with within a week.

Well, weeks passed and 'phone calls were made leading to a further "seven-day notice", assurances that the work would be done "to-night", by "Thursday next week", even that the "work has been com-pleted" – none of this remotely true, of course. The latest promise is that the repair will be made at some time, impossible to predict with any accuracy, but definitely in the future. The clanking gets worse.

And more August complications pile in. We have to visit a friend in Devon who is recovering from unpleasant sounding surgery. Other friends, also in Devon to which they have recently moved, want us to pop down there to admire their new county.

I suggested to Mrs Croft that we persuade them to get together and visit each other on our behalf, thus saving us a long drive, much expenditure on petrol and the planet for future generations. This earned me the familiar basilisk stare from Mrs Croft that leaves me in no doubt that I have crossed one of those invisible lines. So, Devon it has to be. Twice.

One lot of exam results this year will determine whether or not one of our nephews will be showing up at York University in the autumn. Now, Mrs Croft is inclined to indulge her nephews and I have an awful feeling that, if this one's result are what he hopes for, she will take to hanging about the campus with packets of chocolate biscuits like some weird kind of confectionary stalker.

I haven't mentioned this, but I have the feeling that after a few weeks "inter-railing" in Europe he may, having left a boy, have come back a man with an enthusiasm for things other than chocolate digestives. And a reduced fondness for surprise visits from doting aunts.

Planners are undivided on fracking debate

First, the good news. Our nephew, Charlie, achieved top grades in all his A Levels and will be coming to York University in October. He will be many miles from home in leafy Surrey and the warm embrace of his family, but no matter; Mrs Croft is now on the starting blocks ready to bake pies and dispense biscuits. I have suggested that she move into a caravan on the York ring road for more ready access, perhaps with a couple of ponies for company. Poor Charlie – he may have to be careful with information about his precise location.

My sermon this week is about fracking, which promises to be a big feature of this area. It is always difficult to know what to make of such major developments. A friend of mine, a half-mad Old Etonian baronet, always recommends taking a lead from the aristocracy in such matters, but I am far from sure that this is wise advice. Certainly, when the railways came they were hopelessly divided. Half of them bitterly opposed their introduction, chiefly on the grounds that they would encourage the working classes to move about. The rest kept quiet, slyly building spur lines and private railway stations for the exclusive use of their chums, arriving in eager anticipation of enjoying the pleasures of shooting, claret and cold pheasant breakfasts, lark's tongue pate and female domestics. You may have noticed how many names have jumped from the pages of Berk's Peerage onto the lists of those wallowing in wind farm subsidies.

However, the people who are undivided in their enthusiasm for fracking are local authority planning officers. They are all down their legs with excitement at the limitless opportunities fracking provides for them to parade what they imagine to be their business skills and commercial insights and having done so to their self- satisfaction, to come down one way or the other more or less at random.

We are so accustomed to the fact that the country is planted thick with "planners" that we seldom pause to consider what would have happened in earlier times had they then been about their capricious business. No canals would have been dug, no viaducts erected and no coal mines opened up. They would not have been "in keeping", and we would have remained in a pre-industrial revolution slow lane. The working classes would not be moving about and the nobs would be confined to their own landed estates and those of their near neighbours on which to indulge their liking the meat of song birds and other vile appetites.

The absence of coal mines, a valuable source of useful scrum-halfs, would have ruinously retarded the development of rugby union football, especially in Wales, and Arthur Scargill would appear in no volumes of social history written by admiring left-wing academics.

Speaking of left-wing academics, the publication of this year's A Level results has been accompanied by their now annual chorus of dismay that the better universities are doing nothing to increase the admission of "poor" pupils with low results to their degree courses. I fully support their campaign and believe that the principle underlying it should be given wider application. For example, the results of the National Lottery should be tampered with to increase the chances of a win for those, such as me, who are chronically unlucky. This will put an end to what has for too long been scandalous discrimination against those who, although unlucky, enjoy a flutter. Soon we shall see the admission to medical school of pupils whose academic achievements are mediocre, but whose parents don't earn lots of money. This will give a much needed manpower boost to the NHS.

Are your ambitions being frustrated by elitist attitudes? Are you tone deaf and want to be a piano tuner? Get a campaign going.

Books bonanza is a real back-end-of-year treat

Among the usual mouth-watering treats in the back end of the year – Bonfire Night, Hull Fair, my birthday, Christmas – we can all now look forward to a more recent addition to the calendar, and no less glittering; the Ryedale Book Festival. This will take place in Malton on the 19th and 20th of October, neatly placed between my birthday and the day when we celebrate the brave efforts of that other outstanding Yorkshireman, Guy Fawkes.

An extraordinary team of dedicated and talented volunteers, under the inspirational leadership of Sarah Tyson, and supported by a range of local and regional sponsors, has put together a fascinating programme.

There is something here for everyone: children, families, lovers of comedy and crime, aspiring writers of prose and verse. There is even a section called "Events on Saturday for Adults"; before you reach for your grubby mac and low-fitting greasy trilby, it's not what you think, or possibly hope for. For details of this, for other features of the programme, and information about the glittering celebs go to www.ryedalebookfestival.com, or pick up a copy of the brochure at the Malton Tourist Information Centre (TIC) or other locations about town. For some of the events there is a modest charge (tickets from TIC), but most are free.

I should declare an interest here. I have had a minor role, a very minor role, in this enterprise, but much as I would like to take most of the credit the fact of the matter is that I deserve none at all. That is why I can wholeheartedly and without conflict of interest strongly recommend that you pile into Malton during that weekend and prepare to be amazed. Fill your boots.

This event, together with the Ryedale Festival musical events that are put on here, the now well-established monthly food markets and the annual Food Lovers' Festival, is providing a real buzz in the town.

Our newly refurbished town hall, a spanking place, provides an additional attraction to the market area in which the two hours of free parking are a real benefit to visitors. Our corner of Ryedale is a "go to" destination – just up the road there is Pickering, where the Second World War is re-fought annually, there are numerous events centred on the North Yorkshire Moors Railway to pull in families and the steam anoraks.

One does wonder whose side the planners are on in all this. They have permitted the location of "event boards" for the announcement of our attractions on only two of the five approach roads to Malton. Why? The traffic coming this way from York, Scarborough, Beverley, Pickering and Hovingham is substantial and we need to lure in this passing trade, but we are only able to inform some of it.

Presumably there are reasons for their decisions, on the face of it arbitrary, but they are hard to deduce and explanations would help those of us not schooled in the hard science of town and country planning. The Data Protection Act, much loved by officials, may of course not permit this.

One of my favourite spots in Malton is Woodall's, with its Aladdin's cave of merchandise, most of it bizarrely labelled – "a proper thing", "possibly useful" and so on. I noticed recently, when I went in to buy a ball of string, a new line: deer horn whistles ideal for dog training, some of them rather superior, two-tone articles. But I also noticed a two-litre tin, rather plain and marked by the manufacturer "Slapper tattoo ink". Could this, I wondered, be anything to do with York Races where there is always, on Ladies' Day, a fine showing of acres of fake-tanned skin with a top dressing of exotic tattoos? Sadly, no. It is used by farmers to mark their pigs. Oink oink!

Big gathering had a small-party intimacy

Bishop Martin Wallace, the Bishop of Selby, will be retiring shortly after 10 years in office; a service to mark his retirement was held in York Minster. Mrs Croft and I were there along with a thousand other people and a small group of plainly bewildered Chinese tourists who had wandered in out of the rain. I say a service, but it was rather more than that. It was an extraordinary event. In addition to a thousand rubber-neckers there was a host of ecclesiastical nabobs; rural deans, archdeacons, the Bishop of Hull and John Sentamu, the Archbishop of York. All the elements of a church service were there – hymns, prayers, sermon and so on – but the real surprise came with anthems. These were sung by Elvis Presley. How Bishop Martin managed to persuade him out of Essex, where he has a full programme of engagements as you will know from the frequent reported sightings of him opening supermarkets, especially in Colchester, I cannot say, but I can say it was worth the effort.

The presence of Elvis in full show-biz outfit gave an unexpected party atmosphere to the evening, as did a brief comical exchange between him and the Bishop of Hull.

One of the bishop's predecessors, over 50 years ago, confirmed me, when I was a spotty youth with clerical ambitions of his own, fanciful as that may now seem. I considered mentioning this connection to him, but I judged it to be too slender a link, and I'm sure he is constantly on the lookout for stalkers. He would have been still in short trousers at the time, his own acne still in the future, and would then have been startled by any thought that he might one day have to live in Hull. As startled as I would have been by any suggestion that I might leave the place.

I have known Bishop Martin for only a few years, but I have got to know him well enough to detect that his fingerprints were all over the evening's programme. During his sermon he put on a bravura demonstration of his deft sense of humour, which is never far away, and his extraordinary comic timing as he delivered his moving and thought provoking address. It was plain from the many tributes and from the atmosphere among the crowd, most of whom know him far better than I do, that he has been a popular and well-loved figure, and he will be missed.

I have never before been to a party – and a party it was – involving a thousand guests, but the odd thing was that it didn't feel like a big do, but a more intimate affair. That's quite a trick to pull off – having a cathedral church as the venue is a help of course, but it's more than that. I wish him and Di, his wife, well in retirement. Plenty of time now to play their Elvis records.

It was a full weekend, featuring also as it did the Pride of Malton and Norton awards. There was a grand dinner for about a hundred in the Milton Rooms followed by the awards ceremony and, later, entertainment from The Nobodys (sic), a local group. I left shortly after they came on – I always try to slip away before the fighting starts. I decided to add a bit of class to the occasion by giving my dinner jacket an outing, which I soon came to regret because I was repeatedly mistaken for a waiter. It's hard to get these things right.

There were numerous nominees of the highest calibre; as always on these occasions, it was a pity that not everyone could carry off a prize.

I would make a terrible judge because I invariably think that people I know and like should win all the prizes, and it was for this reason, I assume, that the actual judges did not consult me. I was particularly pleased that my friend Andrew Walker of The Patisserie Malton was a winner.

There was an auction, which raised £1,000, during which I made several aggressive bids for a suite for a night in the Talbot Hotel with dinner and breakfast thrown in, but I dropped out towards the end in the face of lunatic bidding from the other side of the room. Mrs Croft looked a bit put out when I fell silent. She had somehow got hold of the idea that she would have been my companion had my bidding been successful.

Local centre for the racing world's injured jockeys

I have just read a book commemorating the 50th anniversary of the Injured Jockeys Fund. This is an extraordinary organisation – a small charity dedicated, as the name implies, to the welfare of injured jockeys. From its early days it has enjoyed royal patronage, first from Queen Elizabeth the Queen Mother and following her death from the Princess Royal.

Its most striking and visible achievement is the development of Oaksey House, a residential facility for the treatment, rehabilitation and care of jockeys. There have, however, been other, less publicised contributions; for example, the swift intervention to support the families of the two young jockeys, Jan Wilson and Jamie Kyne, who lost their lives in Norton at the hands of an arsonist. Oaksey House is situated in Lambourn, Berkshire, a well-regarded centre of race horse training not unlike Malton/Norton.

This project, driven by John Oaksey, faced many problems; raising the finance, identifying a suitable location and securing planning permission. A disused, derelict and rat infested former training stable in the centre of Lambourn, Bourne House, which was no longer viable for use as such was exactly the right place. Donations, many small and some very large arrived in such a way as to demonstrate that, financially at least, it was a practical proposition. Objections came from two quarters: the local council opposed permission for change of use of the premises, insisting against all reason that they should continue to be used for training, and from local people who wanted the character of Lambourn to remain unchanged.

Eventually, Berkshire County Council gave permission for change of use subject to a payment of a little less than half a million pounds to finance affordable housing elsewhere in the county. While it is not uncommon for builders to be required to include in housing developments a proportion of affordable housing, it is hard to see justification for demanding from a small not-for-profit organisation such a huge fee. You could be forgiven for suspecting that planning permission was for sale. In the end this ludicrous demand was withdrawn, Oaksey House went ahead and, after delays caused by archaeological investigations, was opened by Princess Anne in 2009.

The Fund next addressed the need for a similar facility in the north of the country; the obvious location was North Yorkshire, planted thick as it is with racecourses and training stables, with Malton-Norton the front runner. The parallels with the Lambourn project are striking. The planning authority created difficulties, so much so that there was talk at one time that the project would go to Thirsk and that Malton would lose out. There was also local opposition.

Some said that the centre would be better located in Norton, rather than at the chosen site in front of the Malton Rugby Club, on the grounds that it would put the injured jockeys close to their colleagues in the stables there. This overlooked the fact that the users of the rehabilitation services would come from all over the north, not just Malton-Norton and carried the implication that if you wanted to build a centre for injured police officers you would sensibly site it next to a police station, or a facility for injured colliers next to a pit head.

Another objection was that we should maintain the agricultural break between Old Malton and Malton. Much as I enjoy, when walking between the two, strolling alongside a field of barley it is plain enough that this principle was set aside when the Rugby Club was given permission to build there. And many years earlier, on the other side of the road, the corn belt was lost with the building of some fine houses and, notably, the abomination that is Ryedale House. We do not live in a museum and it is foolish to try – but it is a longing that warms the hearts of planners everywhere, chiefly, I suspect, because it affords a neat excuse for stopping things happening.

However, as in Berkshire, so in North Yorkshire – everything was settled. Work has begun, the archaeologists are busy and the expectation is that the centre, to be called Jack Berry House, will open its doors before Christmas 2014. Malton-Norton, like Lambourn before it, will have enhanced their standing as a national centre of racing by hosting a worthwhile and much needed facility for those injured in pursuit of a dangerous sport. If you feel inclined to support this venture you can do so by buying a brick, inscribed on the face with the name of a loved one (or a favourite horse); go to www.ijf.org.uk To read more go to The Injured Jockeys Fund, by Sean Magee.

What difference will 'Culture' title make?
You may have been surprised, as I was, by the announcement that Hull has been declared a City of Culture. I may be wrong about this, but I believe that it has been decided that this is an accurate description of the place now, rather than an expression of intent to turn it into one. It has to said that the competition was less than fierce – Leicester, Swansea and Dundee.

It is true that Hull has one or two jewels in its crown; the Ferens Art Gallery is pretty respectable, as the Hull Truck theatre company, but that's about it. I hear that they are very proud of their enormous aquarium called The Deep, but it's a bit of a stretch to regard keeping a few fish in a tank as a cultural achievement. Some people who came from Hull have enjoyed success in areas of cultural endeavour, but they mostly live in north London. Maureen Lipman, for example. And Tom Courtney, who told me that he never visits the city these days, preferring instead Bridlington. Philip Larkin is dead, of course, and he seems to have hated the place. On the downside there is "Lord" Prescott.

One wonders about the make up of the committee that makes such judgements, and what the competition was this year. If they were able to take historical contributions into account perhaps a few points may have been scored by the city's ownership of the poet Andrew Marvell whose poem To His Coy Mistress excited us when I was a schoolboy there, it being what passed for pornography in that time of innocence. We referred to his collected verse as a "mucky book", a view shared by my chemistry teacher who gave me a detention when he caught me leafing through it.

Referring, as I have, to people who "came from Hull" says it all; people seem keen to leave. When I was a child there the population was a little over three hundred thousand, now it is fifty thousand fewer, a remarkable decline during a period of general population growth. The only sure way of getting out when I was young was to get a place at a university elsewhere. I am sure that many of my contemporaries – certainly it was true of me – only put on a spurt in the sixth form because that was the ticket out, an incentive not available if you grew up in, say, Bristol. One of my less adventurous school friends waited until he was in his late middle age to make a break for it. He moved to Goole. Oddly enough, all the students I have met who moved to Hull's university from elsewhere have very fond memories of the city and many have settled there, mostly to become geography teachers.

We shall see what difference this accolade will make to the city and its residents. I'm sure that the local politicians will be burning off some council tax enjoying self-congratulatory civic banquets in anticipation of inward investment, but I doubt if there will be any street parties along the Holderness Road.

Of course, I am not as familiar with Hull as once I was. I still visit from time to time for family reasons, but I can no longer find my way around with any confidence. I have noticed, however, that the stench of rotting fish is no longer a problem; there are now no trawlers sailing in and out of St Andrew's Dock. Perhaps that is why they built the big fish tank, as an act of nostalgic piety. In the street where I grew up, a street of two hundred houses, no fewer than three of these dwellings had been converted into fish and chip shops and there were at least another four within easy walking distance. Not now, sadly.

I have exciting news on the family front. Daughter Helen, who is due to give birth in the spring, has, thanks to the wonders of modern medical science, been able to inform me that a boy is expected. This will take some wind out of the sails of her brother, Edward. All his cousins are female and all their children are girls. He is inclined to swagger about announcing that he is the only one in the family who can manage to produce male children. I wonder if he wonders in his moments of psychotic self-admiration how he came about.

Santa and Sentamu: a good, but sniffly week

At the beginning of a week filled with high jinx both Mrs Croft and I were laid low by a virus of such ferocity that I almost mistook it for influenza. I had had my 'flu jab as is my invariable practice in late October and, after some badgering from me, so did Herself in anticipation of the shopping trip to Hong Kong. In spite of the well-known term Hong Kong 'Flu, she had not quite taken on board the fact that Hong Kong is where influenza was invented and saw no need until pressed.

Mrs C, crushed by symptoms, took to her bed on Sunday, but rose again on the Monday evening to attend the service at St Mary's to install the new vicar of St Mary's and St Michael's, Peter Robinson, where she read one of the lessons, sounding like Lauren Bacall after knocking back 40 untipped fags. The church was packed with clerks in holy orders – not least of them Archbishop Sentamu – joint choirs and hundreds of sheep. A grand occasion it was. It was followed by a knees-up at the Rugby Club, but we two, virally fatigued, passed on that and went back to bed. Much warming of milk and softening of honey to repair the over-taxed vocal chords.

The following four days found Mrs Croft confined to bed. Her symptoms were reported to be much more severe than mine so my role was not to lie in bed but to be sent out to fetch in increasingly outlandish supplies of over-the-counter snake oil preparations. My main problem was not the symptoms, but sleep deprivation; it is difficult to nod off and stay there when the person next to you is constantly barking like a grey seal and ratcheting away at the child-proof tops of medicine bottles. However, the frequent, unsupervised shopping trips presented plenty of opportunity to pop into cake shops and pick up supplies of cream buns, more effective than Lem-Sip by far.

The Malton Christmas Party on the Friday, held at the Rugby Club, we had to miss, in Mrs Croft's case on doctor's orders, in my case on hers. I try to stay away from the doctor when there is "something going around" because of the risk of coming away with more than you went in with, and I don't mean a prescription. Mrs C took the risk; a quick consultation, a chit for industrial strength antibiotics and these words of reassurance: "Hope you feel better soon! Byeee!! NEXT!!!"

The next day was my big day, impersonating Santa in the Milton Rooms. Conscious of the hordes of excited children expecting to meet me, I dragged my slack old body out of bed, slipped into my outfit and fired up the Morris. During the journey into town I hung out the car window and, tooting the horn, waved at the crowds. I felt like the Pied Piper of Hamlyn, though on a more benign mission, as people greeted me, their faces suffused with delight.

My role in the Milton Rooms, no less sacred in its way than the Archbishop's in church on Monday, was to listen to dreams and to distribute chocolate. The children were enchanting. With very little evidence of shyness and faces shining with such simple belief as Dr Sentamu might, perhaps, have glimpsed among his flock on Monday, they confided their hopes. All observed by slightly anxious looking parents. One little boy, William, scarcely left my side; I think he would have liked to take me home with him. He was rewarded with an extra present.

I had a thoroughly good time. The outfit was a bit of a challenge, however. I managed to dip my beard in my coffee a couple of times and my attempt to eat a mince pie was a bit of a mess – I was flossing with white whiskers for the rest of the day. The difficulties of dealing with a nose that ran like a tap while wearing a false beard are best not described.

So, not a bad week all told. I hope that all the children will be happy with what I leave them on Christmas Eve, though I doubt if the boy who expressed an interest in having a flick knife will be fully satisfied. There's always next year.

Advances in medicine and its practitioners

I may have mentioned before that common medical afflictions when I was a child, such as carbuncles, hunchbacks and Derbyshire neck are now seldom seen. No longer popular, a doctor friend tells me, although I suspect that advances in medical treatments may have had a part to play too. Also you don't hear much about varicose veins these days, perhaps because injections of wax was the treatment of choice, a painful and largely ineffective measure that may have encouraged sufferers to keep quiet about them.

There have been other changes. I have been reading about a popular eighteenth century physician, George Fordyce (1736-1802), whose dietary regime would find little favour with modern doctors. Based on a study of lions at the zoo, he concluded that one meal a day only was ideal in promoting health and longevity. For twenty years after coming to this conclusion his invariably daily practice was to visit Dolly's Chop House in Paternoster Row, close by St Paul's Cathedral, where he would order a one-and-a-half-pound steak, preceded by a starter of half a chicken and a plate of boiled fish. No mention of vegetables that I could find. All this was washed down by a pint of beer, half a pint of brandy and a bottle of port, followed by a large brandy in each of the three coffee houses he would then call at before setting off on his evening medical rounds. He died of gout aged 66 – not a bad score for the time.

His bedside manner was said to have been impaired by his prodigious consumption of alcohol, so much so that he frequently had difficulty in finding a patient's pulse, but his popularity was not diminished. This portrait will not resemble in any way your own doctor who would almost certainly frown upon all that brandy and port, not to mention regular evening house calls. Also, the modern doctor is heavily regulated and probably enthusiastic about vegetable consumption; we are the better for it. One of Dr Fordyce's patients, a wealthy titled lady, was so impressed by his clinical performance when drunk and his polite silence on the matter of her own inebriation that she tipped him £100 (£3500 in our money), an act of generosity seldom experienced today, especially by GPs on their rounds.

During my teens, in the early days of the NHS, I was plagued by carbuncles and monstrous boils (not enough fruit and veg) and I always visited the less popular of our two available GPs. He was an abrupt and rather brutal practitioner, hence his unpopularity, but he was easy to get to see and, unlike his more modern colleague, did not favour the new antibiotics, but was an enthusiastic wielder of the lancet, an approach I preferred: instant relief. Unfortunately, like Dr Fordyce he was also an enthusiastic drinker and finally came to grief when he crashed his Rover into a police Panda car following which he was struck off. Luckily for me I had by this time emerged from the carbuncle stage and no longer needed what would now be regarded as his reckless surgical approach. He was closer to Dr Fordyce than anyone you would come across nowadays.

The reason Dr Fordyce was never struck off, apart from the fact that his professional approach was probably pretty much standard practice at the time, was that there was nobody then to apply such a sanction. Now we have the General Medical Council, a body empowered by parliament to remove the names of delinquent doctors from the register of medical practitioners which is, unusually for such regulatory bodies, funded by doctors themselves. Given that there are well over a hundred thousand registered medical practitioners in the UK, very, very few are dealt with in this way, which means that we are well served by our medics and rightly feel safe in their hands. It is all the more surprising, therefore, that in addition to the boil-lancer of my youth who fell foul of society's disapproval of furious driving when squiffy, another of my GPs, many years later also suffered the fate of erasure. In his case it was for abusing his prescribing powers to obtain supplies of Viagra for his own use, a relatively minor infringement I would have thought. It does go to show, however, that doctors are keeping abreast of advances in medical science, even in matters of misconduct.

I need hardly say, I hope, that none of the events here described took place in Yorkshire.

2014

Educational reformers blinded by equality

January started well. We were visited by my sister-in-law and brother-in-law (Mrs Croft's brother) accompanied by their youngest, Charlie, whom they were delivering back to York University where he is studying biochemistry. His sister, Jessi, is a "City lawyer" (whatever that means) and his brother, Michael, will in a few months be registered as a doctor. They are a high achieving brood by any standards.

All three are, luckily for them, intelligent. Their parents are understandably proud of them, but not on account of their intelligence but for the use they have made of it. I know these young people well, but what I admire most about them is not their brain power, though certainly I envy it, but the qualities of character that have enabled them to squeeze achievement out of it. And their modesty.

I am very fond of telling anyone who will listen, a dwindling audience, that intelligence is no more a moral virtue than is ginger hair, say, which becomes admirable only when it is washed regularly and kept tidy, or height. I have never instructed these three relatives on this important truth – I have been far too busy teaching them to blow their noses and introducing them to the pleasures of cryptic crossword puzzles. But they seem to have figured it out for themselves, and that is impressive; they have taken a short cut across their (comprehensive) school playground and arrived at the conclusion it took me much longer to reach.

The trouble with educational reformers is that they are so blinded by zeal for equality that they quickly lose sight of the fact that not everything can be fixed by legislation.

The luckless Michael Gove is a case in point. To be sure, he cuts a ludicrous figure on the political stage, but his heart is in the right place, albeit with an irregular beat.

But he will be defeated by his confidence that restructuring and diktats will overcome vital underlying inequalities in matters of education: deft upbringing from parents who "get" education, qualities of character and, not to be sneezed at, the availability of caring uncles who understand the importance of skilful and timely deployment of the handkerchief.

This is not to say that intelligence is unimportant – like many genetically endowed qualities, ginger hair and so on, it is; but these are gifts not achievements. There are lessons in this for politicians and educationists, many of whom are themselves intelligent, if only they would listen to me. Not everyone can be a High Court judge or a David Beckham, though there is no harm in trying on a wig or picking up a football just to see. Take my own case. My physical beauty has been frequently remarked upon, ever since the spots cleared up anyway, but I would be unlikely to win many prizes in competitions where all the judges valued only ginger hair, or indeed hair of any kind. However disappointing this may be, I cannot in all honesty say that it is unfair.

I have made an approving reference to modesty in paragraph two, but I should add a minor amendment; a codicil, a lawyer would say and send you a bill for fifty guineas. My nephew (the doctor) left school, like his siblings, with a becoming degree of personal modesty. However, modesty is not a quality much prized in the medical profession and I have noticed that somewhere during his six years of medical training his tutors have excised it like a suspicious lump. They had their reasons, and good reasons they were I am sure, but there is always the danger that opportunistic hubris might creep in to replace it.

Ever aware of my avuncular duties, whenever I see him I pass him a handkerchief and, with much exaggerated sniffing, point to my nose – just to keep him honest. It would be a great irony if he turned out to be an E.N.T. doctor and, albeit small, a contribution of my own to the future of medicine.

Archie's hero - with flat cap, big coat and 'tache*

My seven-year-old grandson's class will be "doing" heroes this and they were instructed to turn up on the first day disguised as their chosen idols. It must have been quite a sight at the school gate that morning as the young snipes reported for lessons. All the usual suspects were represented, with much duplication: David Beckham, Harry Potter and so on. You get the picture.

But there, tottering along behind, was young Archie in flat cap, ill-fitting coat, and false moustache, with spotted handkerchief hanging from his pocket and brandishing a special dog walker's stick (incorporating a useful whistle). His hero? None other than your faithful scribe – his grandad.

This was quite a boost for me, coming as it did only days after the disappointment (again!) of not finding my name on the New Year's Honours list. I can see where David Beckham is going wrong, but the Establishment's repeated refusal to acknowledge my life of distinguished service is utterly incomprehensible, and a possible indictment of its integrity.I gather that Archie was not prompted by his father in his choice of hero – no surprises there – which makes this recognition all the more heart warming, and certainly worth more than the measly CBE that I have been denied twice a year for so many years.

I must say that I am very impressed by Archie's school, Peppard Primary, in Oxfordshire, and not for the first time. They demonstrate an interesting and innovative approach to education that was entirely absent from my own infant school. They would certainly never have pulled a stunt like this, encouraging their young charges to show up disguised as their role models.

A very different crowd it would have been then, of course: Denis Compton, himself honoured by HMQ for services to Brylcream, Lord Baden Powell for scouting for boys, and the Archbishop of Canterbury would all have had quite a following, with Bernard Montgomery in strong contention.

Peppard School scored high marks in my book for insight and sound judgement when Archie's class teacher, impressed by his unexpected, inter-generational choice, declared his effort to be excellent and invited him to present his reasoning to the entire class of Beckhams, Harry Potters and assorted pop idols.

His reasoning, in effect a citation, reads as follows: "My hero is granddad. This is because he is a newspaper writer. He sends it all over Malton and over to Daddy and another for me. It has funny comments and my Dad thought it was funny. I thought it was funny but I did not think it was as funny as me. He has a squashed moustache and a bald head with bits of hair sticking out." Everyone's a critic, even seven year-olds.

But it did the trick. He was given a Superstar certificate to take home for the fridge door, and an extra one for me, for my fridge door. This school should be excused Ofsted inspections for at least a decade and given an increase in its budget for that thoughtful gesture alone.

I visited the school in November, on Archie's birthday, to collect him and take him out for a meal. Never having been there before I wanted to check that I was at the right school so I parked and approached a woman at the gate (she had the look of a teacher about her) and the following exchange took place:

Me: Is this the only school in this area with Peppard in the name?
Woman: Do I know you?
Me: I don't think so. I'm not from these parts.
Woman: Are you famous?
Me: No.
Woman: You look as if you might be. Are you off the telly? Are you sure you're not famous?
Me: Well, not unless you read the Malton and Pickering Mercury.
Woman (clearly not convinced): Oh.
I wonder who she told her husband she had met that day. Alf Garnett probably.
See back cover for picture of Archie as grandad

Patients and pupils are terms of the past

Belting it with the family Bible having failed, I took my ganglion to a converted chapel in York where orthopaedic surgery is now carried out. There I discovered that the NHS has now forbidden surgeons to operate on ganglia, for reasons unknown, but my hand was X-rayed anyway to confirm the diagnosis. Luckily for me it turned out not to be a ganglion at all but a Brown's tumour. Whether the "managers" at the NHS consider a Brown's tumour to be a graver affliction than a ganglion, the word tumour having made them nervous, or simply haven't heard of it, I cannot say (I suspect the latter). I shall be "going under the knife" some time in the next few weeks. I can't help thinking that assessing relative risk should be left to the doctors.

In the short time I was in the chapel I was asked several times if I would be able to manage the stairs. Considering the fact that I had "managed" the steps to get into the building in the first place and had skipped nimbly up to the reception desk it seemed it bit unnecessary. I see the fingerprints of Health and Safety all over this, who have decreed that all patients, no matter how spry and how good a bet to make through another night should be questioned in this way.

I say "patients", but I have become aware recently that we are no longer referred to in the NHS as such but as "service users". Doctors and nurses are, I suppose, service providers now and that soon prescribed medicines will carry the advice "If you experience any side effects go and see your service provider". I don't like this. My service provider is the chap who checks over my car every 10,000 miles; it is my doctor who checks me out, with similarly depressing results.

It is the way with large bureaucratic organisations with reputation management problems to tinker with language to avoid improving substance. British Rail was among the first to come up with this dodge, dropping the word passenger and substituting customer, hoping to assure us that BR staff see us not as passive freight but as discretionary spenders to be treated with respect. In schools the children are no longer pupils but students, indicating, it is hoped, that we shall detect in this a respect for the little blighters not previously evident. Nor are they children any more, but young people.

But back to medicine and health. In a single issue of my morning paper no fewer than three medical breakthroughs were reported. (1) Men who sleep soundly at night have a 75% lower risk of developing prostate cancer (Harvard Medical School finding). (2) Consumption of chocolate and red wine leads to a decrease in the likelihood of diabetes (University of East Anglia). (3) Smoking during pregnancy increases the possibility of the baby turning out to be gay (University of Amsterdam).

Prostate problems have become fashionable recently, and certainly they are increasingly popular among my contemporaries. It may well be that there is an association between poor sleep and prostate cancer, but as difficulty sleeping is not uncommon in men over 60, I doubt if a causal link will be found. Very clever chaps at Harvard though, so you never know.

Several years ago it was announced that taller men are more likely to develop prostate cancer than short men. I wonder if there was a rush of lofty fellows piling in to that chapel in York requesting that a few inches be trimmed out of their shins. I shall ask when next I am there.

I do not take seriously anything coming out of the University of East Anglia, not after their odd behaviour around climate change research.

I worry about the Dutch. Finding causes always implies in medical investigation the possibility of prevention or cure; I doubt if gay activists will be very happy with this research no matter how much they may deplore smoking during pregnancy. There may be demonstrations.

Also, it is my experience that women on the whole like gay men and enjoy their company, so there is a risk that pregnant women may take up smoking in order to encourage the birth of sons who will have more attractive personalities and be kinder to them than the general run of men. Who knows?

Pointy head lunacy over dredging issue

Finally, the penny seems to have dropped concerning the useful-
ness of dredging rivers and other watercourses. It always seemed
to me that it is counter-logical to assert that allowing arteries to silt
up and narrow would not increase the likelihood of flooding.

Blame is flying about like snowflakes in a blizzard. "Lord" Smith is
doing sterling work defending the Environment Agency's frontline
workers, highlighting their dedication and so on; he is right about
that, but it is not they who are being criticised, it is the pointy heads
at the top who dictate policy, and he is Pointy Head-in-Chief.

The trouble started when the universities started offering courses
in "environmental science", which is not a science at all but a belief
system, and their graduates, bird watchers and vole fanciers all,
gradually insinuated themselves into the outfit and ousted the
drainage engineers and hydrologists who had for so long supervised
the dredging.

I doubt if the Agency will survive with its "flood" portfolio intact, if
it survives at all. No doubt superannuated "old school" engineers will
be dragged out of retirement to get us back on track; I hope that they
will charge like wounded elephants when setting their fees.

Two items reported by the press beautifully capture the mind set
of the tree huggers. One, discussing the Somerset Levels situation,
explained the matter by making reference to what things were like at
that location 10,000 years ago. What possible value or enlightenment
is supplied by that sort of talk?

At that time the Welsh had not discovered the secret of woad.

The second is a report of a lecture given by a pointy head from the
Agency in which he confided self-righteously that culling mink is
suspended during their breeding season in order not to upset animal
lovers.

Why not delay winter 'flu jabs until the spring in deference to the
virus's right to family life? The argument put forward (by a pointy
head) against the re-introduction of dredging is that the silt and
other detritus dredged onto the banks would be categorised as
industrial waste (by the pointy heads), the removal of same requiring
a licence. Such licences are issued by the pointy heads, who say they
would refuse to issue any.

Thus they have created a self-serving closed loop of their own
lunacy which they hope will protect them from the need to re-
introduce a process that they don't understand and that they believe
will make life difficult for wildlife.

It seems to me that they underestimate the opportunism and

versatility of wildlife. There is a corner of the largely unspoilt stretch of the River Derwent between Malton and Old Malton that is marred by the hand of man.

Beneath an abandoned and derelict stone railway bridge there is a pool littered with masonry, broken bottles and other trash and yet it is there that kingfishers can most reliably be sighted.

The other villains in all this flood misery are the local authority planners who persist in ignoring advice, and go ahead and give permission to developers to build on flood plains and other sites susceptible to flooding. This could be dealt with by a simple change in planning law, easily drafted.

All planning officers and council members should be obliged to indemnify in perpetuity all future residents and owners of such permitted buildings by surrendering the deeds to their own houses in the event of future claims.

Re-mortgaging would be an offence punishable by incarceration. They should also pledge half of their pension funds in the same interest, and commit their first born children to working for minimum wage on community interest projects.

I have considered a reintroduction of the death penalty for reckless planning decisions in respect of flood risk, but I don't want to appear harsh. (I have noticed that Wentworth Street car park often floods. Has anyone told Tesco, I wonder?) Anyway, my little law would put a stop to their foolishness. It could be called the Croft Amendment.

There would be plenty of defaulting, of course; sly re-mortgaging, creative use of trust funds and feigning death and insanity, these latter two not requiring much acting talent.

New prisons would be needed for such people, in which case the Croft Amendment would be waived in respect of such building projects – if they are built at Spurn Point and on the cliffs near Hornsea. I rest my case.

NHS in crisis? Think back to the old days!

It is a common feature of advancing years that things start going wrong with our bodies and we find ourselves more frequently being sent to hospital specialists. Apart from relief from in my case minor but nevertheless embarrassing personal ailments, visits to the hospital provide interesting opportunities to observe what goes on. During the last few months I have enjoyed vantage points in two out-patient departments: head and neck surgery, and hand surgery.

Newspapers report almost daily that the NHS is in meltdown, and it is true that there are problems, but things are in many ways much better than they were when my parents were going through their periods of chronic malfunction before the Grim Reaper finally showed up. For example, they would attend an appointment with the specialist, who would decide that X-rays were called for. Another appointment would have to be made, weeks later, at the radiology department, following which, again weeks later, there would be a return visit to the specialist to find out what had been revealed. Not always, but very often, the X-ray films would not have arrived; the hunt would then be on, and sometimes they would be declared "lost in the system" and it would be back to square one.

It is very different now. If X-rays or other simple imaging techniques are required you are sent off to radiology, pictures are taken on the spot and back you go to see the specialist again. By this time, maybe 20 minutes later, the images are on the computer screen to be viewed by patient and doctor together, with the doctor explaining what he or she can see and what it means. Not so in the old days when nothing was shared, little explained. One hospital visit for me, at least three for my Dad if he was lucky and his X-rays had not gone astray.

I noticed an interesting difference between the two departments I have been dealing with, both at the same hospital. In the case of one, following referral by my GP, I was sent a letter asking me to telephone to agree a date and time for an appointment. One letter, one phone call. In the second case I received a letter asking me to telephone to let them know when, during the anticipated waiting period, I would not be available, following which a second letter would be sent offering two dates from which to choose, which I could do by making a telephone call. Two letters, two telephone calls. If, having received the offers, I found that neither was possible for me I would be discharged back to my GP and a second referral would have to be made. Literally rusticated.

Now, reading two letters and making two telephone calls is not an especially burdensome requirement for me, being retired, in fact it makes me feel rather wanted. But someone at the other end has to write these letters and receive my calls, and there are thousands like me.

The second system, apart from being less efficient, has built into it the threat of rustication which instantly doubles the administration at the hospital and gives my GP another opportunity to see me, which I am sure he could happily do without.

In my recent experience of the second system the first letter helpfully informed me that the anticipated waiting period would be

314 months.

This is a little over 26 years, considerably more than Dad was ever faced with in the Bad Old Days. It is more than likely that in 26 years from now the Grim Reaper will already have introduced himself to me; the surgeon too, judging by the shape he looked to be in at the first appointment. It was, of course, an error and not an attempt, as I cynically at first thought, to set targets that couldn't be missed. The letter should have read 3-4 months.

On another subject, equally important and troubling, is why do the makers of shirts assume that as your neck thickens with age your arms grow longer? Is it the case that, to avoid this tricky question, shirt makers are increasingly sizing shirts not by collar size but S/M/L? And why am I now a large? I am built like a jockey's whip, though rather powerful of chest which may be the problem.

Trip for frock-shopping and celeb-spotting

A trip down Memory Lane took Mrs Croft and me to London last week, primarily for a briefing at the Garrick Club by jockeys and trainers ahead of the Cheltenham Festival. I say primarily because as it turned out there was a hidden agenda – shopping for frocks, a retail opportunity in which I was not permitted to share. I cannot explain my exclusion; I would have thought that, with my nose for a bargain, I could have made a valuable contribution, but apparently not.

We stayed at the Groucho Club, a louche establishment in Soho, recently mentioned in the telephone hacking trial as the watering hole favoured by Daniel Craig and Jude Law where one of them behaved less than honourably. You may have read about this in the yellow press. I am no longer a member of this club but Mrs Croft lingers on in the hope, I suppose, of catching a glimpse of James Bond. The Groucho has always been favoured as a top hole spot for observing celebrities with their guard down and in the past I would entertain there distinguished figures from the world of medicine in the hope of persuading them to write a book. It would make a change for them from places like the Garrick Club where they would normally park their broad bottoms, and where retired lawyers and written-out novelists are what passes for celebrity.

I was reminded of one such occasion when, at breakfast, I spotted Lenny Henry a couple of tables away, nibbling a rusk and working feverishly at his laptop. Years ago a professor of medicine asked me to take him there so that, he shyly admitted, he could report to his impressionable teenaged children that he had hobnobbed with people they might have heard of. We arranged to meet in the bar and, as he was as usual late, I perched on bar stool to dazzle the staff with my wit. The chap on the adjacent stool turned to me and asked if I had a pen he could borrow, and I was able to oblige.

Eventually the medic arrived, thirsty from saving lives that day, and we stayed a while at the bar and just as we were about to move on to the restaurant the man without his own pen came over to return mine. We exchanged pleasantries and that was that. Later, towards the end of the meal, my companion complained that he had not spotted a single famous face. What about the chap who'd had my pen? It was – you are probably ahead of me – Lenny Henry, but all he had noticed was the black face. Mortified, he raced back down to the bar, but the joker had gone. I advised him to lie to his children as they, no doubt, lie to him. He had, after all, looked at Mr Henry even though he had not seen him.

Anyway, back to my day out. While Mrs Croft was in Knightsbridge giving the London economy a boost I mooched about in Old Compton Street looking at the changes since my last visit. (It was on Old Compton Street, you may remember, that I was made a most unsettling offer by a wandering transvestite.) I noticed a new café-cum-deli called Maureen's Kitchen and I pressed my nose against the window to assess Maureen's offerings. It all looked very tasty but when I saw the price of a scotch egg – six quid, if you can believe it – I instantly lost my appetite. £1.18 at Fletcher's, note.

The evening at the Garrick went well, I thought, and Mrs Croft assures me that the tips she picked up for Cheltenham would more than match her extravagance in the frock shops earlier in the day.

She may be right; she certainly bets large on these occasions, none of the thirty bob each way that I venture. We shall see. I did notice, however, that her confidence in future winnings was not such that she tried to stop me paying for dinner.

I would like to report that I spotted a few celebs in the Garrick, but I did notice across the bar an old friend, Tim. I made my way across the room to greet him; luckily, I remembered just in time that I had attended Tim's memorial service a year ago – or was it two? – and managed not to make a fool of myself.

Perhaps I had seen a ghost. So many members of the Garrick look as if they have been dead a while.

Various bans – but I maintain my innocence

L ast week I travelled to Hull to attend the funeral of the mother-in-law of a friend of my childhood, Dave. She had died there at the age of 95. Almost 50 years ago she reacted badly to the fact that, having enjoyed a Christmas lunchtime drink with me and a few others, Dave returned to her home where he was staying a touch squiffy. So squiffy was he that he was unable to join her and her family for an evening with her relatives, but took to his bed, not to be heard from again until Boxing Day.

Her disappointment was understandable, as was her dilemma; having promoted Dave as an ideal son-in-law to the entire family – "golden boy" may have been a term she used – she could hardly admit that she had made a faulty judgement of his character and now denounce him as disgusting wine bibber. Someone else would have to be found to take the blame. Step forward young Howard. Her version of events, a complete travesty of the truth, was that I had taken advantage of his innocent nature and led him into error.

This was, to me, an unconvincing theory; he was, after all, older than me, blonder and, a quality much prized among mothers-in-law in those days, taller.

In order to make her feelings crystal clear she uttered this interdiction: "Don't bring that bloody gyppo into this house again!" Her very words. They may shock you. These days, of course, she would in short order have found herself in front of a magistrate for using such language, and I would be trousering a few thousand quid for my hurt feelings

But my feelings were not hurt. I had never made any secret of the fact that my grandfather was a gypsy and I was rather proud of him. He had come back from the Great War, having left behind at Ypres one of his legs, and resumed his career as an all-in wrestler in spite of his disability which he would later claim was no disability at all but an asset. It would make his opponents reluctant to move in for the kill.

I also admired his enterprising practice of "borrowing" ponies from a field next to the pub to take him home whenever he was one over the eight and his stump was playing him up. I hope to meet him again some day, on another road.

Anyway, I never did visit again the home of the recently deceased lady, although I did meet her occasionally at other locations and she was civil enough.

Her husband at such times took to drawing me aside and telling me unbelievably filthy jokes; this I took to be a token of his regrets at least that I had been banished for life.

This is not the only experience of being banned from domestic premises that I have endured. The wife of another friend, a highly strung woman to say the least, on discovering that her husband had overdrawn at the bank, swiftly came to the conclusion that I was in some way to blame. She subjected me to close interrogation about my financial practices, wanting to know in particular if her husband and I were in the habit of lending each other money. I explained that this was so, that we would sub each other with the odd fiver from time to time in the company bar at lunch time (those were the days) if one or other of us had not managed to get to the bank. She asked me, indeed told me, to give a solemn and binding undertaking never again to behave like this.

I refused to give any such undertaking, pointing out that if she could successfully instruct her husband never again to slip me a fiver I would quite understand, but that if he were to find himself a bit short I would always help him out. She reacted with great fury, and I confess that for a few moments I was acquainted with great fear, for I knew that she from time to time knocked him about a bit during episodes of marital disharmony and I thought she might start in on me. She did not do that, but she did ban me for all time from the marital home and that ban is still in place to this day.

There may be some among you who think they can detect a pattern in all this, but that would be uncharitable of you and it would do you no credit to put such a theory about.

A day at the races, and nights avoiding the bidet

A busy week: a day at Cheltenham for a spot of racing, a day in London attending to weighty matters and a weekend in Caversham visiting son Edward and his family. Grandson Archie, who publicly declared me to be his hero and won golden opinions for doing so, has rumbled to the comedic potential of my hearing aids. His sister, Imogen, not quite three, he still regards as a bit of an interloper and, explaining her shyness, dismissed her saying, "She doesn't recognise you, she doesn't know who you are. Anyway, you are here to see me". So, not so golden after all.

Cheltenham was fun, as it always is. It is interesting to note how serious, wealthy race-goers all dress alike. The women in togs apparently made from horse blankets, topped off by trilby hats tricked out with game bird feathers and martially booted below. The men, also in trilbies but plain, with jackets a couple of sizes too small – are tight jackets a fashion among the horsey set or evidence of advancing corpulence and a vain refusal to face up to it?

Aware of Mrs Croft's extravagant betting, I placed only small bets and few of those. In anticipation of my forthcoming grandparental visit, with all the demands on my wallet that would entail, I ventured a few quid on a runner called Granddad's Horse in the hope that it would supply the necessary funds. It failed to do so. Mrs Croft claimed to be a hundred up on the day, but no audit was permitted so this may not be an accurate final figure.

The weekend finished on a sad note; two of them, in fact, both deaths. I was greatly saddened by the passing of Tony Benn whom I met and got to know slightly when I was an undergraduate in Bristol and he was our local MP. This was during the time when I fancied myself a socialist. He frequently came to the university to address us, and to endear himself to us by discarding his jacket and tie, then an uncommon and radical posture, and by strutting about, red braces on show (always red, I remember), spouting dangerous ideas.

Many years later, when I was living in Notting Hill Gate quite close to his home, I ran into him in the local Marks & Spencer food shop and I reminded him of those days – there we were, two elderly gents reminiscing about a time when we both thought we might amount to something. Much to the irritation of his minder, his son (now of course Viscount Stansgate), who was clearly more interested in getting the old boy to make a decision about a prawn cocktail for his lunch.

The second death was that of my sometime boss in Nigeria, Chief Felix Iwerebon – also, like Benn, gathered in full of years. He was an extraordinary man who saw plotters everywhere; not even his wife was above suspicion. It was his belief that she had two mothers and he claimed that their prolonged stays in his home were for the sole purpose of driving him into bankruptcy by eating vast quantities of eggs from chickens he kept in his back garden. He would frequently summon me to his office to describe his domestic difficulties, always kicking off with the words "Now, Howard, my wife Joko is a difficult woman". I once jokingly suggested he take legal action against them, which to my consternation he did.

The grandiose plans for his funeral, no doubt of his own devising, will give you the measure of the man. "1st May, Service of Songs; 2nd May, Commendation Service; 9th May, Service of Songs II; 10th May, Lying in State, followed by Funeral Service; 11th May Outing Service". Outing service?

He had many eccentricities, most of which I personally witnessed, but one of them – which I was never able to verify – was rumoured to be a novel use of his bidet. This he regarded as the ultimate accoutrement of refined western living, and there is no denying that. But the use to which he put it is seldom to be practised in the genteel homes of aristocratic English families on whom he sought to model himself. He would, it was said, thaw out packets of frozen peas in it and, when having a party, use it to bring bottles of wine to just the right temperature. Tony Benn may have had a view on this, but it's too late to raise it with him.

I went to many parties at Felix's home in Lagos, and in his flat in North London, but I always avoided the wine and never accepted peas.

Rules and regulations for my post-op safety

I have had to visit a hospital in York for a pre-operative briefing. I had thought that the removal of a ganglion-like growth on my trigger finger would be rather less of a performance than the root canal work my dentist did recently. Not a bit of it. One of the many forms I have filled in so far asked for my occupation; I was tempted to write "Army Sniper" in the hope of better service, but I don't really look the part. Judging by the briefing, and the documents I have had to read, it is very much more of a performance.

I have been instructed to report for duty at "no later than" 7.30am, and told not to expect with any certainty release before tea time. There will be some expense involved. I am to take slippers and a dressing gown. As my slippers were eaten by the puppy months ago and my dressing gown is, according to Mrs Croft, not fit to be seen, I shall be sent shopping, taken probably. There are risks attached to every stage of the procedure, ranging from the possibility of a mild headache up to quadriplegia and death, all comprehensively listed and described. I am beginning to wonder if I should bother. I am not, after all, an army sniper and unlikely to become one, notwithstanding my late-flowering fantasies to the contrary stimulated by newspaper reports of a soldier in the British Army polishing off, "slotting" is the technical term if I heard Prince Harry correctly, five enemy fighters with a single bullet.

Having cranked up my anxieties with doom-laden documents, they then piled it on further by explaining the terms and conditions of my release. I half expected to be told the name of my probation officer. I had been planning to drive myself home; who does not drive wearing a finger stall? This will not be possible as my upper torso will be shrouded in bandages and my hand lashed to my shoulder.

Thinking aloud in front of the nurse, I pondered my alternatives. It just so happens that on the day I go under the knife Mrs Croft will be in Hampshire attending a funeral that cannot be missed, and one of my spoken thoughts was to take a taxi to York railway station and jump on a train. This is not permitted – no taxi driver would do; someone must collect me in a car. But a taxi is a car and a taxi driver is someone, surely? But no, a taxi driver cannot take responsibility for me and they would not entrust me to one. I know several cab drivers in Malton who would, I am sure, gladly help me out and they are – I'm sorry to say this – a good deal more responsible than many of my friends, some of whom even have degrees from quite well known universities.

I was surprised by this regulation. One of my neighbours, an elderly lady living alone, was put in a cab at Scarborough Hospital and sent home where she arrived cold, confused, hungry and miserable at one o'clock in the morning. Had it not been for her alert neighbours, and their kindness, I shudder to think what might have become of her. They fed her and kept her warm until proper arrangements could be made the next day. And yet I, fit as a fiddler's bitch and more or less intact mentally, cannot be trusted to find my own way home and wait a couple of hours or so to return from her day out and rustle up a fry-up. I didn't mention the possibility of a fry-up, by the way; they would probably have sectioned me under the Mental Health Act.

I was considering my options the following morning as I walked the dogs – should I attempt to put together a complex set of arrangements, or concoct a tissue of plausible untruths, or simply, come the day, slip out and hitch a lift – when I was saved by another dog walker, and friend. Jessica, also known as the wolf woman (she has a white German shepherd), as soon as she heard the story instantly offered to be my carer for the day. She will have to pose as my daughter, I think.

If I am spared and anything interesting happens, you'll be the first to hear about it.

Shovelling money at the BBC incompetents

It has been very interesting to watch over recent months the growing unpopularity of the television licence, not only among those who pay it but those who benefit from it. It has never been exactly popular with the public, but accepted; increasingly now they resent it. The beneficiaries, having loved it once no longer do because it is increasingly possible legally to avoid paying it while watching BBC output on iPads and mobile telephones, though why anyone would want to watch telly on a mobile is beyond me.

Suggestions that the BBC should move from a licence fee to a subscription model of funding have been made, but the BBC itself has been rather lukewarm on the idea. Pious reservations have come out of Television Centre about a two-tier system that a subscription model would probably bring about and that would be, in some unexplained way, "unfair". These sanctimonious hand-wringers conveniently forget that they themselves, years ago, introduced a two-tier licence fee – one for black and white tellies, a higher one for colour. The truth is that they know that a subscription service would find them out. In the days of Lord Reith, and for many years after, those who ran the BBC saw themselves as public servants. Their integrity and their concern to produce high quality, uplifting content was seldom, if ever, questioned. This cannot be said of the current bunch: venal, self-serving, and secretive and, if appearances around the Jimmy Savile affair are anything to go by, dishonourable. Oh, yes – and incompetent.

Now we see why they have been talking down the subscription idea; they have a better wheeze. They are proposing a television poll tax, a universal levy payable by every household including those who have no television set, iPad, computer or mobile phone capable of tuning in. A sort of cultural tithing.

This, they think, would be fair. There can be very few who never watch television and have no means of doing so, but there are some, and they must pay up anyway under this proposal.

I for one think it is a splendid idea, worthy of wider application. We could, for example, make every adult over the age of 17 pay vehicle excise duty irrespective of whether or not they own a car or hold a driving licence. What could be fairer than that?

There could be local versions, administered by councils. Lots of scope there; annual rat catching fees for those with no rats, planning fees for those with no plans.

If you think these are the implausible rantings of an unhinged Faragist looney, remember this: it is not long ago that nice Mr Clegg proposed that all graduates should pay interest on their student loans for the full permitted term even if they were lucky enough to pay them off early.

Further, if they were lucky enough not to need to take advantage of a student loan they should nevertheless pay interest on the money they had not borrowed. More equal is more fair.

He could have added that children with two parents, which is obviously unfair on those with a lone parent, should be required to murder one of them just to even things up, but I think that even the

LibDems would have been uncomfortable with that.

So, let the BBC tax us all. They certainly know how to spend. They recently sent a team, sixty-five strong, to film a programme on lambing and accommodated the lot in a luxury hotel for four nights at £275 a night, total over £70,000, plus of course dinners and wine, probably an extra £15,000. They justified this on the grounds that it was the only hotel near enough to the location of the shoot that could lodge all sixty-five. It does not seem to have occurred to the clever suits at the Beeb that they didn't all have to stay in the same hotel. Perhaps they were all sleeping with each other and it was judged to be good for morale to make shifting alliances possible without shuttling between hotels.

So, perhaps we should continue to shovel money at them in any way that suits them and we can watch their antics when their snouts are in the trough, occasionally raising their heads briefly to pay each other obscene amounts in severance before rehiring them the following week. And to make the odd TV programme, why not. If they still no how. Now, is Pointless on tonight?

Telephone heroics, and a hero in medical world

For reasons related to American tax authorities, too complicated and boring to rehearse, Mrs Croft and I have a substantial wedge of cash lodged in a NatWest foreign currency account. For reasons unexplained NatWest have unilaterally decided to close all such accounts at short notice. Because the US dollar has declined in value against sterling I am keen to keep it in dollars in expectation of a more favourable exchange rate in the future.

Luckily, I have a relationship with another bank, Lloyds, to whom I could turn in my hour of need. Or so I thought. My Lloyds account, at the Malton branch, is now a TSB (though still owned by Lloyds) and a thoroughly efficient and helpful outfit it is, but it does not offer international currency accounts. However, I do still have so-called "private banking" arrangements with Lloyds so off I went to York. I was taken under the wing of a young lady, Sophie Tustin, who instantly grasped the issues and set about trying to get hold of the right person in their "international division".

I sat there for about an hour as she tried to locate the right person. She was given number after number to ring, none of them of any use, and on several occasions she listened to a recorded message telling her our position in the queue. On every occasion, as soon as she heard that she was first in the queue, the call was automatically transferred back to the "phone bank", ie the switchboard. This happens after any wait of ten minutes. Eventually, she received a solemn and binding undertaking from someone that I would be called at home later that day. No-one called.

Another visit to the bank followed with more telephone heroics from Sophie resulting in success. A charming young fellow who wanted to be known only as Malcolm contacted me and skilfully guided me through a complicated procedure, and solved my problem. We are all horribly familiar with multiple menus when trying to get hold of any human being, never mind the right one, in a large organisation, but it was instructive and amusing to watch a determined young woman battling her way through her employer's system in order to contact a colleague.

I concluded from this that there is not much wrong with the people in Lloyds Bank, but quite a lot wrong with the unhelpful systems put in place by their employer. I wonder how much time is wasted by staff simply trying to locate each other. A case of deploying technology just because it is there. More pencil-necked geeks at work.

I have been reading about a remarkable man called Henry Miller, a Tyne-sider who qualified as a doctor at King's College Durham (now the University of Newcastle) where he remained for pretty much the whole of his career. He specialised in neurology, became Professor of Neurology, Dean of Medicine and, finally, Vice-chancellor of the university. He died at the young age of 62 in 1976.

I never met Dr Miller though I heard a lot about him from, among others, John (later Lord) Walton with whom I had a long association as a medical publisher. John's career almost exactly mirrored that of his mentor, Henry Miller, apart from the Vice-chancellor role. Such was the fund of anecdotes about the man that, following his death, the British Medical Association published a book, long out of print now, entitled Remembering Henry, a copy of which I recently acquired. Here are two stories.

Driving at excessive speed to visit a patient, he realised that he was passing a police car. With great presence of mind, he snatched up his stethoscope from the passenger seat and waved it through the window of his car at the officers. On his return journey he saw the same police car; as he drove past the policeman, grinning broadly, waved his handcuffs at the good doctor.

All neurologists possess a stick with a rubber wheel at one end, and a fine point at the other. The wheel is used to smartly hit a patient's knee to make the leg twitch. The point is used to stroke the sole of the foot which should cause the foot to clench; this is called "evoking the plantar reflex". Henry, a keen motorist, taught all medical students that "the only satisfactory way to evoke the plantar reflex is with the ignition key of a Bentley motor car".

If you are interesting in reading a very amusing book about a re-markable man, second hand copies can be bought on the internet (via Amazon). The authors are Lock and Windle. You may have to pay as much as £1.75 for a copy in good condition.

In a onesie with Spice Men was festival treat

This is positively the last bulletin on my finger. I know how worried you have been, but I sense that you may also be getting rather bored. I was summoned to Clifton Park Hospital for a post-surgery review at which I was scrutinised by not one, but two nurses whose entire field of expertise is the hand. The operation was declared to have been a success, but some residual side-effects were discussed.

My trigger finger does not fully curl in when I make a fist. Clearly, this was my fault in that I followed an exercise regime recommended to me by a GP friend when we were walking our dogs in Hatfield Forest. Quite wrong, I was told. So much for GPs and what they know. Superior exercises were prescribed and I was told that there is every possibility that full flexion will be restored in "weeks running into months". It was also recommended that I should go about with my hand raised as this will promote a reduction in swelling. I pointed out that it would also promote the idea that I am in perpetual need of the toilet with helpful passers-by directing me to the nearest public convenience, any teachers among them adding the stern caveat, "Oh, all right. But only if you are quick".

There are two other problems; loss of feeling and susceptibility to cold. Feeling will be restored "sometime next year", but only if I keep my hand elevated and exercise diligently. It was explained that this problem is not the surgeon's fault. I had discussed the numbness over a warming bottle of red with a rheumatologist friend with whom we stayed last week and he said that feeling would probably never return. So much for rheumatologists. But – he may be right; thirty-odd years ago I had abdominal surgery and the loss of feeling around the scar (also not the surgeon's fault) is still with me. We shall see.

The susceptibility to cold ("only to be expected") was easily dealt with. Wear gloves earlier in the winter, ideally mittens but socks would do. I have not worn mittens since I was at primary school (tethered by wool passed through the sleeves), and socks on my hands only when out snow-balling, now, of course, a prohibited activity. Ski gloves were also recommended. All very technical stuff.

So I was discharged, in cracking shape, "back to your GP"; I felt like a prisoner being released into the care of his probation officer with a similar feeling that good behaviour is expected. I shall do my best.

For those who, like me, find that with advancing years there is a loss of vocabulary the constant introduction of new words is a constant challenge. How to keep up? There are pitfalls lying in wait, a recent example of which made me look foolish. An old friend of mine, Saira Hamilton, was scheduled to do a cooking demonstration at the Food Lovers Festival, but sadly was unable to be here because of the unexpected death of her father just hours before she was due to leave for Malton.

The television chefs the Spice Men, of whom Saira is a great admirer, were at the "gala" tasting dinner in the beautifully refurbished town hall, presumably having heard that Mrs Croft was going to be present. Thinking it might cheer Saira up at an otherwise difficult time I came up with the wheeze of having a photograph taken of Mrs Croft with the Spice Men and get someone to twitter it to her (I don't twit). I approached the Spice Men's minder to ask her if she could arrange for this to be done, saying "Could you fix it for Mrs Croft and the Spice Men appear together in a onesie for Saira to see?"

What I meant, of course, was a "selfie". The prospect of Mrs Croft and the Spice Men being bundled into a onesie and sent off to Saira must have been a startling idea, but without batting an eyelid the minder quickly interpreted my wish. I looked a fool, but was not made to feel one.

The tasting dinner consisted of six courses – very small portions, but excellent food. A friend of mine, a trencherman noted for his fondness for rib-sticking courses generously plated up, commented, "It's not really a meal, is it? I have never been so glad to see a broad bean on my plate."

For those, like me, who have more modest appetites it was a delight. If you missed this Festival, be sure to catch the next. It is a real asset to Malton – the food capital of northern Europe.

Beware Black Wednesday!

Just when I was beginning to hope that political correctness and mindless regulations had begun to recede, two particularly ludicrous examples caught my eye in the Daily Telegraph. A leading neurosurgeon, Mr Henry Marsh, announced that he had taken early retirement from the NHS because he had been forbidden to wear a wristwatch in the hospital. His employer had issued a 22-page dress code probably aimed, though he did not say so, at reducing hospital acquired infection. There is, he said, no evidence that wristwatches cause infection. Given that wristwatches were invented and routinely worn by hospital staff long before the epidemic in recent years of such infections I suspect that he is probably correct, though I am not a microbiologist. Will hospital visitors be turned away from the wards, much as those carrying flowers already are, if they are wearing wristwatches, even have them confiscated?

I was reminded, when I read this report, of the diktat that came out of Brussels several years ago banning, for reasons of food hygiene, the use of wooden chopping boards in restaurant kitchens. Instead they insisted on the use of four colour-coded composite boards – red for meat, green for vegetables, white for poultry and blue for fish. As far as I know this was not based on any evidence, and failure to comply could, and often did, result in restaurants being closed down. Subsequent laboratory tests conducted by microbiologists demonstrated that composition chopping boards are significantly more likely to retain dangerous organisms than wood, both having been scrubbed in hot water. The regulation has never been rescinded.

The second report is of a church putting a hoarding in its grounds bearing the words "So you don't believe in God. Let's hope you are right", beneath which there was an illustration of a fiery inferno, a depiction of hell. This was not an especially subtle message, though there was some humour in it, if not much. One person complained, the police investigated, the display was recorded by the police to be a "hate crime" and down the poster came.

One wonders what the police were thinking, in the first place "investigating" this complaint and, secondly, deciding that hatred was in any way involved. From the point of view of Christians, not many of whom these days subscribe to a view of hell more popular in the Middle Ages than now, this warning would be seen as an expression of love and concern for their fellow men who, like sheep, have lost their way.

I am sorry that the church concerned caved in and took down the notice. "See you in court" would have been my reaction, though I doubt that any sane prosecutor would support the police and dare to take such a case to a judge, but this sort of nonsense needs testing judicially.

Where will it end? On this principle, "Caution – ice on road" could be interpreted as a hate crime, or "Beware of the dog". "The end is nigh!" might also attract the attention of the police if mounted on a sandwich board and paraded around Hyde Park Corner.

However – some good news. My nephew the medical student is now my nephew the doctor. He came third in his finals out of 370 students in his medical school and was awarded two medals for excellence.

I don't know what it is about doctors and medals; they are forever giving them to each other, they're as bad as the army. No-one ever gave me a medal.

So, all these young doctors will be looking forward to the first Wednesday in August when they will be dumped onto hospital wards and told to get on with it.

This day, when every year the number of hospital deaths shoots up, is known by the medical profession as "Black Wednesday" and by patients as "The Massacre of the innocents". Only the arrogant among them will show up for work on that day without feelings of anxiety to say the least.

Good luck to them all – and to us too, of course.

D-Day 'escapee' Bernard deserves our admiration

The outstanding feature of the events commemorating the 1944 D-Day landings in Normandy was the contrast between the Chinese New Year pyrotechnics put on by the French and the moving lone piper tribute paid by Britain. Including, for now, the Scots. It was no surprise that the French show featured a German and a French serviceman, with little reference to Britain, America or the Commonwealth countries, most notably Canada and Australia.

The runner-up contribution was the effort made by 89-year-old British veteran Bernard Jordan who, in spite of his care home's failure to get him to France, managed to find his own way there and who as a result stole the front pages of all the papers. He was feted as a hero on his return to Blighty where he received more attention than it is likely he enjoyed when he returned sixty or so years ago.

His behaviour was of course highly irresponsible. It is unlikely that he carried out a full risk assessment before setting out to the ferry port, or that he made a written record of that assessment. It takes little imagination to picture the fury of his carers, and the social workers in his area, who will no doubt be closely looking into matters in spite of their smiling faces when the cameras were rolling. The possible complicity of his wife, with whom he lives in a care home, also bears close scrutiny. It seems to me that he deserves a medal to add to those already pinned to his chest, but in these more enlightened times he will probably be sectioned under the Mental Health Act. More grease to his elbow, I say, and to his wife's if she knew his plans and kept mum.

Whatever lunatic decisions the "authorities" arrive at in this matter they will require the support of the police. As it was in the case of the parents of a 10-year-old boy who were arrested and charged with child neglect when it was a discovered that he weighed an astonishing 15 stone. It is true that this child is in big trouble health-wise and that without some sort of intervention he will have a short and unhealthy life. But intervention by police officers?

The medical profession is finding it difficult to do anything about the obesity crisis, which involves so many factors, and they are not helped by the changing advice handed down to them by the health authorities. At one time they were told not to use words like "fat" and "obese" as such language would upset people and damage their self-esteem, but instead to use terms such as "unhealthy weight". Then they were told to use such plain language, freely using "fat", "obese", "chubster" and the like on the grounds that euphemisms would be unlikely to command the necessary attention. Who would be a GP or practice nurse with this sort of contradictory stuff flying about?

Far better, in my view, to leave it to the clinical judgement of medical professionals to decide, on a patient-by-patient basis, the best approach. I had a personal experience of this situation when I turned myself in for my annual medical MOT. When it came to the weighing-in I was slightly anxious because Mrs Croft had told me I had been been losing weight, with all the possible sinister implications of that. But also, if she were to turn out to be correct, there was the exciting prospect of maybe digging out my old flares and loons from the Seventies, carefully mothballed and kept in anticipation of a switch in fashion to more retro styles, when I would again be able to cut a dash.

I stepped lightly onto the weighing machine and waited for the verdict. After years of constant weight I was told that in the past 12 months I had put on a pound. So much for Mrs Croft's eye. The nurse expressed only mild concern, suggesting that I might consider possible ways of arresting this unwelcome trend; fewer peach melbas, perhaps, or a little more exercise? I was happy to have this discussion. Had she, on the other hand, said "Now look here, Mr Croft, you're turning into a right porker and if you don't mend your ways you'll be a diabetic in no time flat and be facing a painful early death", I would have been less co-operative and would probably have checked myself into the nearest mental health facility complaining of low self-esteem. Messages from Whitehall are always worth ignoring in my view; nurse knows best.

Need the loo? Can you wait until the morning?

My theme this week is waterworks. I did not know until recently told that the public conveniences in Malton market place close overnight from five o'clock in the afternoon. Not very observant of you, I hear you cry, and you are right. In my defence I should say that I do not spend my time hanging about public toilets (an occupation known in London as cottaging and, by Mrs Croft only, as "bungalowing") and memorising opening times.

The suggestion has been made to an officer of Ryedale District Council that the closing time for these facilities could to some advantage be extended to 10 o'clock. Many objections were raised, not least the problem of who would lock up at 10 – a dangerous time, according to the Council representative, especially on Fridays and Saturdays.

A reliable and responsible local worthy offered to undertake this duty himself, but this was instantly ruled out of the question on the grounds that he has not been trained for this role.You may wonder what training and of what duration the Council considers would be necessary to qualify someone to lock a toilet. And, indeed, who would provide it. I wonder if this difficulty was raised by the same Ryedale House employee who tried to stop me sweeping up leaves outside my house on the grounds that I had not been trained. You may remember me mentioning this surreal episode before.

The logic of shutting the toilets at teatime is not obvious. I suspect that it is (a) convenient for home time at Ryedale House, (b) fear of vandalism or, (c) a belief that there is no demand in the evenings. Or a combination of these. (a) I understand perfectly – we don't want our public servants overdoing things – but (b) and (c) are more of a challenge. I do not look at the world through the eyes of a vandal, but it seems to me that these premises are pretty vandal proof and, being in an enclosed space, offer little attraction to the toughs who lurk on Friday and Saturday evening who, by their nature, like their mischief to be on show.

As for lack of demand, I doubt if this is true. There is no evidence that I am aware of that bladders, dodgy or not, miraculously cease to make demands on the stroke of five. They are no respecters of the clock and can, like dodgy clocks, strike at any time. I have noticed many times at around five coach parties of elderly people piling back on board after a day's feverish shopping in Malton, anxious to return to such places as Beverley, Doncaster and Selby. These people will probably want to "go" before they go and if denied the opportunity may take to vandalism of their own.

Many councils (not RDC as far as I am aware) have suggested that local food and drink outlets in towns and villages should make their toilets available to visitors, and so enable the authorities to make savings by shutting public conveniences. It is hard to imagine the proprietors of the Dickens of a Deli say, or the Hidden Monkey welcoming hordes of tourists piling through their door with no intention of spending money, apart from a penny of course. I doubt if the councils who back this potty idea would be willing to make the facilities in their offices available for such use. Don't hold your breath, hold your water.

More on waterworks, though of a different kind, next week.

In the meantime let me share with you the transcript I read this week of a call made to the emergency services:

Operator: How can I help you?
Caller: I have been stabbed.
Operator: How many times have you been stabbed?
Caller: Er....this is my first time.
Aren't people wonderful?

A fuel such as I – diesel error proved costly

The weekend away began very well and ended disastrously. It got off to very good start with us hidden among hundreds of mums and dads watching their children graduating from being medical students to becoming doctors. Hundreds of them, too, but we had eyes only for nephew Michael and his squeeze Chloe. Such a brief transition after six years of hard work.

The ceremony had the feel of a BAFTA Awards evening, in part thanks to the appearance of Jonathan Ross on a video show urging the new graduates to join the University College London Alumni Association. It came as a surprise to me that Ross had himself been educated at UCL, indeed it had never before occurred to me that he had been educated at all. Why I should have been surprised I cannot think; after all, I knew that Mick Jagger, a popular singer from the Sixties, had attended the London School of Economics.

The students took their cue from Ross's appearance, prancing on to the stage and waving at the audience who responded with whoops of approval and shrieks of joy in a most un-parental manner. I responded with a dignified scowl and frequent furtive glances at my watch. Many times. Once let out of the auditorium these new doctors, gowned and hooded – the hoods, appropriately blood red – enjoyed themselves for several hours striding about in their finery and downing glasses of wine in greater quantities than my own doctor would allow. It seemed to me likely that many proud parents would have difficulty coaxing their offspring out of their robes at bedtime.

In the evening we were treated by Michael's parents to a fine dinner at the Oxo Tower restaurant, a place I used to frequent before I retired and could no longer afford their prices. It was a tiring day that started at 11 in the morning and ended close to midnight.

The following morning disaster struck. When I went to refuel the car I was so exhausted that I overlooked the fact that it has a diesel engine and put in unleaded and drove off, causing thousands of pounds of damage. There is nothing intrinsically amusing about this incident, but news of it has been greeted with hilarity by family and friends, and even by strangers who seem to have got wind of it. The only possible conclusion I can reach is that humour has been found not in the error itself, but that it was I who committed it. So much for loyalty.

When I arrived home, after a difficult journey that took a circuitous route in order to avoid the infestation of Lycra-clad cyclists who should by rights have been in France, I found a grim communication from the Driving and Vehicle Licensing Agency. You are, it said, on the very verge of reaching 70 (years, not MPH) and unless you complete this form you will no longer be permitted legally to drive a car. The form requires me to certify myself free of no fewer than 21 medical conditions, some previously unknown to me.

Working on the principle that if I had never heard of an ailment I couldn't possibly be suffering from it, these were quickly dealt with. Others I could easily check – a glance in the mirror was enough to confirm that I don't have only one eye, for example. I did pause, however, when asked whether I have "a problem with memory or periods of confusion", the filling station episode being still in my mind, but I cleared myself on the grounds that I could remember it.

The question about "persistent alcohol misuse" required careful thought and sober reflection, but I was again able to give myself the OK. "Attacks of disabling giddiness" troubled me for a while (the petrol pump again), but, with that one settled, I was able to sign myself right across the board. Fit as a butcher's dog, me.

Had "night terrors" featured on the list it would have been a different story.

Falling foul of Ryedale's brown refuse bin racket

If, like me, you signed up to the brown bin racket and paid your twenty-seven quid you may, also like me, have been shocked that Ryedale District Council's intention was that, should you move home within Ryedale you would be obliged to cough up again in respect of your new digs. Shocked and disgusted possibly, but not surprised. This condition was not spelt out, or even referred to in "small print" (a dodge popular with dodgy traders) when the scheme was "sold"

This blatantly unfair, and I suspect illegal piece of chicanery came to light when one Coleen Guest moved within Malton a few weeks after forking out her twenty-seven hard-earned and was confronted with a further demand in respect of her new address. Wisely, and not fearful of being branded a "moaning Minnie of Malton", she reported her outrage to Councillor Luke Ives. Mr Ives clearly knows a con when he sees one and he sprang into action on his constituent's behalf and had the policy reversed.

The Leader of the Council commented on this matter with a lack of grace that only Conservative politicians seem able to manage. Agreeing that the policy is unfair she reportedly said "It is standard practice among local authorities to apply green waste subscriptions against the property, not the person, so this change will take us outside of the norm, although it will result in a policy that is fairer and it will benefit our green waste subscribers." But only if they move house, of course.

It may well be true that all local authorities have adopted this until now concealed and larcenous policy, or "norm" as Mrs Cowling puts it. But just because it is a "norm" doesn't make it right, or legal, which I suspect it is not. I understand that it is a "norm" among thieves when they burgle your house to help themselves to the contents of your refrigerator and enjoy a bit of a snack. Norm does not equal right.

I wonder if Mrs Cowling, or the genius who devised this new way of picking the pockets of rate-payers, has considered what norms prevail outside the bizarre world of local government. When you pay for a television licence, which is also address specific, and you subsequently move house, the fact that you are still paid up is registered at your new home provided you let the authorities know where you have gone. I assume that when Mrs Cowling moves house she will tear up her TV licence and start again from scratch.

This property specific point is entirely bogus. Any service that you pay for to be delivered to your home is yours not that of your house; a subscription to a journal is an example. It is portable. And so is, or should be, the collection of waste. The purpose of the plastic tag on your wheelie bin is to enable the bin men, or operatives as we now call them, to verify quickly and reliably that the person at the address on the tag has paid for the service they are delivering.

Other points come to mind. What if someone living alone were to die after paying his £27? As he will no longer require the service, which is delivered periodically, any unused but paid for service should be returned to his estate and for accounting purposes should be treated in the Council's books as a liability, a balance that reduces as time goes by. What if you leave the District altogether, what then is the "norm"; do you receive a refund? If not, does the new occupant inherit the paid for service? Have these things been considered by the geniuses, or simply "not mentioned" in the prospectus?

It is interesting that the Council refers to the payment as a subscription, an odd term to choose, I suspect without fully understanding the implications. This is an area in which I have had, as an academic journal publisher, experience and some expertise. Did the Council envisage a one-time start subscription, for which there are rules, or an any-time start, for which there are different rules governing what you may do with reducing balances in hand and your obligations to your customers. I imagine, if they thought about it at all, they had in mind a one-time start, but they would run into difficulties with new arrivals in the middle of the season and finish up with an any-time start system. In other words, a mess out of which ad hoc concessions will not provide an escape. Trading Standards, please note.

These are technical matters familiar to publishers of serial publications and to secretaries of membership organisations, but probably not to town hall wallahs who may not have consulted their legal colleagues. I would be happy to advise free of charge. Plus VAT.

Doing Christmas twice – in English and Danish

Christmas this year will have some convenient circumstances and at the same time some complexities. The plan is that my daughter

Helen, is coming to visit with her family and, as chance would have it, she is married to a Dane. Conveniently, Danes celebrate the season on Christmas Eve. For them, Christmas Day is very much business as usual in much the same way that Boxing Day used to be for the Scots.

This means that Helen and her lot can do the Danish thing on Christmas Eve and then, the following morning, shoot up the A1 to join us in Old Malton. The "Danish thing", which I have never witnessed myself, involves circling round the decorated tree and, holding hands, dance about while clearing throats in Danish. At some point in the proceedings there will be a knock at the door announcing the arrival of Santa Claus who will skip about and distribute gifts to any children present. Just one per child – careful people, the Danes.

The scheduled arrival of our guests on Christmas Day means that we shall treat it like Christmas Eve (English style) and pretend that Boxing Day is Christmas Day with stockings hung by the fire the night before and the usual events the following morning. Mrs Croft likes a Champagne breakfast as a rule. It's all very confusing. As I said to Mrs Croft, I shall be at my wits' end by the end of it all. "Well", she remarked, "you won't have had very far to go." Nice.

An additional complication comes from the second visitation by Santa. How will he know to come to Old Malton, on the wrong day, to visit the grandchildren who, according to his records, live two hundred miles away? Can we pull it off and does it amount to fraud? During a family conference about this it was agreed that I would drop Santa a line giving him the new delivery address, a strategy that was heartily endorsed by two year old Maggie. She wants sight of my letter and a copy of any reply that I receive. It will be a difficult letter to write. How to begin? "Dear Santa, you may remember me from the time I last wrote to you in the early Fifties ..." might do the trick.

I am very much enjoying spending time on the cliffs by Sewerby; very bracing, sometimes a bit too bracing. I found up there an educational display, placed by East Riding Council, describing and explaining the Battle of Waterloo, my favourite battle. It is very well written, lucid and to the point, easily understood by any but the dullest teenagers. I did notice, however, that there were nine occasions calling for an apostrophe with seven of them totally lacking this useful mark. Two, however, did carry the required apostrophe, but both were incorrectly located.

I have never understood why people find apostrophes difficult, but it is plain that many do. Even less comprehensible is how a local authority, whose staff are on the whole well educated, can put out a document like this so riddled with errors (there were others in addition to the nine apostrophe solecisms). Why don't they get someone to proof read written material, preferably someone who paid attention during English lessons at school?

For several years I received written communications from a young woman employed by the North Yorkshire Police Authority. She obviously knew that there are such things as apostrophes, but was completely clueless about the use of them. Her practice was to sprinkle them about her writing, almost invariably incorrectly. I pointed this out to her and offered to tutor her, but she airily dismissed the matter as being of no importance. She had obviously resigned herself to ignorance. She was a graduate, by the way, which is a depressing thought.

My final brown wheelie collection, to which I was entitled as a loyal "subscriber" to this service, and I now have a few months to decide whether or not to renew my "subscription" next year. I am in two minds, partly because the period ended before the leaves had all fallen, and partly because of the restrictions – "not transferrable", "no refunds" and so on. I have been told unofficially that no substitutions are permitted, that is the practice of neighbours offering their spare capacity to each other. I have been unwittingly delinquent in the matter during the leaf fall and I fear that I may be receiving a Long letter from the authorities. It's a vexing business.

Baldness – apparently I'm in denial and unwell

As some of you may have noticed, I am almost completely bald. The balding process started when I was in my twenties and was pretty much complete by the time I was 35. So, for half my life and a greater proportion of my adult life I have been what is termed by classically educated people striving to amuse "trichologically challenged". It is not a matter to which I give any thought and I have never experienced any mockery because of it, though occasionally junior members of my family ask questions, out of genuine curiosity, such as "Why does your forehead go so far back?" The prophet Elisha was not so lucky; the Old Testament records that he was mocked in the street by children shouting "Go up, thou bald head!"

Driving back from the coast yesterday I tuned into Radio Four – I still think of it as the BBC Home Service – and caught a fascinating programme on the subject of male pattern baldness. It is a condition that is in the process of being medicalised. I am now a hair loss sufferer. It seems that many people, mostly charlatans but not all, are making money out of offering solutions; pharmaceutical, surgical and cosmetic.

Many years ago it was discovered that a medically prescribed drug, a beta-blocker, was found to promote hair growth. The trick was to crush into powder tablets provided by doctors to treat hypertension, stir it into a solution to create a paste which is then applied to the scalp. It is important to wear surgical gloves when applying the paste to avoid the possibility of vigorous hair growth on the palms of the hands. It is not recorded what first prompted this experiment. Similar claims have been made for a drug licensed and prescribed for treating enlargement of the prostate.

Currently under research by serious clinical scientists for the treatment of asthma is a new compound which is being offered for sale on the internet, conveniently in powder form, by reliable traders in the Philippines, China and elsewhere. This substance is not licensed anywhere in the world for therapeutic use.

Several hair-loss sufferers were interviewed on the programme, all of whom represented themselves as seriously disabled by their condition. Depression was frequently mentioned, as was low self-esteem. One, who referred to hair loss as "cancer of the spirit", claimed that he would be happy to die if only he could have "two good years" (with a thick head of hair), and another confessed that he was unable to venture out of his bedroom. People who, like me, accept their baldness with a shrug and the attitude "it's just one of those things" were accused of being in denial and assured that they are unwell, probably seriously.

Most surprisingly, it was reported that some men have hair implants without their wives knowing of it, disappearing without explanation for the procedures, often for a couple of weeks, and do not account for the ten-to fifteen thousand pounds taken from their savings. One fellow who routinely wore a wig (wigs are now known as "hair systems") had been married for many years without his wife being aware of it. You can't help wondering about that relationship and about the astuteness of the wife.

Some serious research is being done at the University of Pennsylvania into people's perceptions of men with and without hair. Photographs are shown of men with vigorous growth and assessed for several qualities – age, height, attractiveness to women and so on – and later the same men are depicted, by doctoring the photos, without hair and similarly assessed. The results show that the hairy ones are judged to be more attractive (of course, but I don't think Yul Bryner and Sean Connery ever had much trouble getting dates), significantly younger, two inches taller and, whatever this means, fifteen percent "stronger".

I have decided not to worry about this. I may, of course, be missing a trick. Perhaps if I sold my car and invested in surgical implants things might improve. For example, when checking into a hotel on a business trip, I might find air hostesses running amok in my room, desperate for my embraces and fainting with desire. I doubt it somehow.

I think I should consult my doctor. It is a well-known medical fact that taller men are statistically more likely to get cancer of the prostate; is it likely, I shall ask him, that if I were to sport a hair system and thereby increase my perceived height by two inches would my prostate be at greater risk. He'll know.

R.I.P. Maggie, a woman with pioneering spirit

My mother-in-law, Margaret O'Flynn, died in late September at the age of 94. She died peacefully in her chair after eating her lunch and enjoying her customary glass of wine, the latter not referred to in the obituary that will appear in due course in the British Medical Journal.

Margaret trained and qualified as a doctor, unusual for a woman of her generation, during the Second World War, going on to become a specialist in gynaecology. When I met her she had retired from medical practice but she was for me a rich source of stories about a time, well before my own. She was trained in gynaecology by John Peel, later Sir John, who became the Queen's gynaecologist and who remained a friend of Margaret's until his death in 2005 at the age of 101. All four of her children were delivered by Sir John, a source of great pride to them all. He took pleasure in telling the adult Mrs Croft that he was "the first man to see your bottom".

Margaret trained at King's College Hospital Medical School, London, where, after a brief evacuation to a place of safety (Glasgow, not often so described), she completed her medical education. Many casualties of wartime bombing were taken to King's and she spoke often, with the clarity of recall that often comes with old age, about her experiences then. She described the chaotic intake of the dead and injured and painted a chilling picture of a row of four desks behind each of which sat a doctor; their sole duty was to complete and sign death certificates.

Medical students and junior doctors were asked to perform clinical tasks for which their training and experience scarcely prepared them and which would doubtless horrify their modern equivalents, although I have no doubt that they would rise to the occasion if called upon to do so – which I hope they will not be.

There were also non-clinical duties to perform. When London was being bombed, before the casualties began to arrive, these juniors were organised into two teams; one team would be sent on to the hospital roof with brooms to sweep away the incendiary bombs onto the ground below where their colleagues were waiting with stirrup pumps and buckets to put them out.

But her favourite stories were always about the social life she enjoyed in wartime London; the parties, the balls and the outings. She could remember the dresses she wore and when, the men she danced with and why, and the reputation she enjoyed for having "the finest pair of legs in King's College" to which she frequently referred. I think she cherished this distinction more than any other, more even than her Fellowship of the Royal College of Obstetricians and Gynaecologists (rare for a woman at the time), a goal she achieved before her husband, John. They were the first married couple both to hold this Fellowship, although there may have been others since.

I doubt if an unsophisticated Yorkshire man was what Margaret had in mind as a suitable husband for her youngest child, viewing me as Miss Havisham viewed Pip – those coarse hands and thick boots, or in my case green suede shoes, which she told me never to wear in the Home Counties. I never mentioned this, but I thought it a bit strong for someone with origins in Stoke on Trent to take a sniffy attitude to my neck of the woods.

Be that as it may, we became good friends and I enjoyed her company very much indeed, our friendship based in part on a mutual love of her daughter and a shared suspicion of the Conservative Party. Her passion for shopping, an enthusiasm she passed on to her daughter unfortunately, remained to the end – only a week before her death the pair of them went out to the shops where she bought five blouses and a pair of shoes, none of which she ever wore.

Her funeral will take place in Hampshire where she raised her family and where she transformed the provision of health services for women, particularly in the field of fertility management. We are expecting a contingent from Ireland (her late husband, John, grew up in Galway), a group who understand what makes a good wake. If you hear that all police leave is to be cancelled in Hampshire during the second week in October, you will know why. RIP Maggie O'Flynn– may light perpetual shine upon her.

2015

Why over 400 attended funeral of farmer Jos

It can be dreary in January and February and all of us one way or another devise strategies to see us through to March. Mine is to go into a fugue state, load up the wine rack and hope for snow to brighten up the landscape. My brother-in-law and his wife claim to be spending the whole of January in Burma, though it could be that they have exaggerated and are doing a holiday relief job at a Burmah petrol station, living in a rented caravan behind it. Mrs Croft, of course, goes shopping.

This is less of a problem now that she has discovered internet shopping because most of the "must have" frocks go back. The latest item was a great floral number that made her look like Kew Gardens on the move and at the try-on put me in mind of Burnham wood.

However, this year she has decided that, as our DVD player is on the blink, we should get rid of it as well as the telly, which is working fine, and buy new. Her co-conspirator in the reckless enterprise, Gavin at TVC, has persuaded her that he can supply a telly equipped with Loose Tooth at little extra cost, an app that will enable us to watch programmes on our Eye-Player before they are even broadcast, meaning that we shall no longer need a DVD player. Money will be saved.

The old telly, which I still think of as our new telly, was sold to her not many years ago by my son, who was upgrading to a fancier model, and I seem to recall that she paid him for it the amount he had given when it was new. Another bargain. Our new-new telly has a much larger screen. So large, in fact, that we shall have to buy a couple of gay-glow shell suits to wear when we are staring at it.

This January, however, no amount of frantic retail activity and wistful hoping for snow could even begin to offset one dreadful event – the sudden death of John "Jos" Sturdy at Eden Farm, Old Malton. He was a farmer, rugby enthusiast, sometime columnist on this newspaper, amateur poet and skilled pie maker and hare jugger. His passing has had a profound effect on this community the like of which I have never before witnessed.

His funeral at St Mary's Priory, the church he had attended and served since he was a child, was an extraordinary affair, a local version of a state funeral. Well over four hundred people came. Every pew was filled, including the choir stalls, every space crammed with people happy to stand to pay tribute to this remarkable man. A fellow pupil from Pocklington School delivered a eulogy that was as well-crafted as it was eloquently delivered. It was long, but no-one wanted it to end.

Although we knew him for only a few years, Mrs Croft and I owe Jos a particular debt. When we moved into Old Malton eight years ago he was the first to knock on our door to welcome these new outsiders and to invite us to a game supper in his kitchen at the farm. He expected his old friends there that night to budge up and make room for some new ones, which, because it was Jos I suppose, they happily did. Many such invitations followed over the few years left to him.

From time to time Jos showed up in our kitchen and always, when asked what he would like to drink, a thoughtful expression would appear on his face and after a lengthy pause he would brighten up and say, as if such an idea had never previously occurred to him, "I would like a gin and tonic. A large one!"

He was a kind and thoroughly decent man, and great fun to be around. He is, and will continue to be much missed. May light perpetual shine upon him. I don't doubt it.

Harmless activity under the cosh from council

The Old Malton Oldies' Wine Tasting Club, following a grim hiatus, has come back stronger than ever; twenty-four enthusiastic bibbers turned up gravely to assess nine South African wines. We had some problems during the first incarnation. A public spirited local resident complained to the district council about the excessive noise generated by us as we left the Memorial Hall at nine in the evening. The combination of wheezy farewells and the rattle of Zimmer frames so late at night was too much for some.

The council dealt with this matter promptly and sensitively. "Go get a life" seems to have been the message, but expressed of course in courteous and diplomatic language.

This incident did, however, have an unfortunate consequence: it drew to the attention of the council the fact that we were indulging our hobby without a liquor licence. Relentless and stern in its guardianship of the public good, the council decreed that in future we should obtain on an ad hoc, per diem basis appropriate permissions, for a fee of course.

Sadly, this rendered our activities financially unviable. We were driven to behaving like persecuted Catholics during the reign of the first Elizabeth, meeting secretly in each other's houses and visited, not by recusant priests to celebrate mass, but by roguish wine buffs with a taste for risk. Although we did not go so far as to install priest holes where they could hide if we were raided, I did have plans drawn up for a cupboard behind my wood burner where we could brick-up with a case of vinegary wine any expert whose jokes might be wearing thin. Paul Tate Smith, say. However, the strain became intolerable and we decided to have a break.

Until last week, when we reconvened at a secret location to evaluate some pretty indifferent Cape wines. I noticed across the table a couple of ladies, Megan and Lesley (names changed to protect the guilty), who were helping themselves to wine in quantities in excess of what would normally be required for judicious tasting. As the evening wore on they treated themselves increasingly generously and I became anxious lest disorder might set in. "I say, ladies," I said in my best head-masterly tone , "this is a wine tasting, not a booze up." "Well", says one, saucy as you like, "in that case I'm in the wrong place!" I thought, but did not say, the place is right enough, but I do wonder about some of the people. I doubt if those recusant priests had to put up with this kind of lip. It was a good evening, however, though the wines were mostly awful. Should you spot some figures, stooped and cowled, hurrying through Old Malton under cover of darkness, be not afraid, these are not ghosts of Gilbertine monks, but us, making our way to a booze up.

I must say that I do not understand the attitude of the council to our harmless activity, attempting to squeeze licence fees out of us. Rather, I should have thought, they should view our wine club as an unofficial faculty of the University of the Third Age, or U3A as those of us in the know call it. We are learning about wine varieties and educating our jaded palates and at the same time having a jolly good gossip.

There has been much in the press lately about loneliness and isolation, particularly among those of riper years, and, inexplicably, local councils have been given a leadership role in addressing these problems. I do wonder where they will find the time for this, busy as they are with dealing with obesity and managing how much salt we sprinkle on our cod and chips. The simplest thing would be for them to give us a grant, which would enable us to meet more frequently and to buy fancier wines. Job done, I would have thought.

Farewell Rev Quentin, a loyal new-found friend

Making new friends in later life is not, in my experience at least, as easy as once it was. The instinct effortlessly to engage with new faces seems to fade, and certainly the instant recognition of future potential seldom kicks in. In 2010, when first I met Quentin Wilson, I was fortunate to know at once that here was someone I wanted to know much better. I was attracted by his donnish sense of humour, his unfailing cheerfulness and, as time went by, I came to value his friendship, loyalty and his non-judgemental nature.

The Reverend Dr Quentin Wilson, to give him his full title, died on February 16 at St Catherine's Hospice, Scarborough, following a long period of often harrowing treatment for cancer, which he bore with good grace. Throughout the difficult months prior to his death it was plain to all who knew him that his overriding concern was the burden his predicament was placing on his wife, Anne, whose devotion to his care was unflagging and exhausting. It is for her that we must now concern ourselves.

Before coming to St Mary's, Old Malton, to hold the fort during a long interregnum prior to the appointment of the Rev Peter Robinson to the joint benefice of St Mary's and St Michael's, Malton, he had enjoyed a varied ministry. One of his first posts was in the East End of London where he numbered among his parishioners the Kray Twins, successful and, in some circles popular, gangsters. He went on to more salubrious locations – Exeter Cathedral, Windsor and ... Burnley! He was, I suspect, more comfortable in the company of others with musical talents (he was an accomplished organist and an enthusiastic chorister) than that of East End gangsters.

On a personal note, I very much enjoyed his sermons, which he delivered in a relaxed and conversational manner, deploying engaging humour and always without the use of notes. Although a man with scholarly gifts and inclinations (he successfully completed a PhD thesis at an age when most people are coasting into retirement) he did not overburden his congregations with recondite Biblical exegesis more appropriate to the pages of the Expository Times, preferring instead more accessible material. From time to time he inserted references that only I would pick up – private jokes, if you like – with a mischievous smile. It was, and continues to be, my belief that he did this in order to find out if he had my full attention, and to secure it on future occasions. It worked.

He and Anne were blessed with a happy and supportive marriage and there was always a warm welcome at their home in East Heslerton, which they shared with their much loved cat, Kitty. I bet they were up all night for several nights before coming up with that name. During his final days at St Catherine's a framed photograph of Kitty was in place on his side table.

Having discovered Quentin's fondness for confectionary, I often took cakes when I went to visit – he was particularly partial to iced fondant fancies from Betty's. On one occasion I took a box of four, three of which he, Anne and I dealt with and later, when I had gone, Quentin carefully and accurately cut in half the remaining one which he and Anne shared.

St Catherine's Hospice is a remarkable place and I was greatly moved by the loving care that Quentin and Anne received there in an atmosphere of calm, kindly and attentive professionalism. Visits were always sad, but Quentin's stoicism and pawky sense of humour were there to the end.

Quentin Wilson: diligent priest, devoted husband, loyal friend and cat lover – may he rest in peace, bathed in light perpetual.

Child development: it's mostly in my genes

It is a common temptation for parents and grandparents to believe that their grandchildren's sayings and achievements are endlessly fascinating not only for close friends, but also for complete strangers. I well remember a woman ahead of me describing to a stunned check-out girl, in greater detail than was strictly necessary to make her point, a perfectly executed infant bowel movement. Myself, I subscribe to the motto "mum's the word".

I have, ever since I became a grandfather, firmly believed that credit for outstanding intellectual, social and personal development such as I see every day in my own grandchildren should be scrupulously attributed. The causes are multi-factorial. My observations have led me to the conclusion that five percent is due to deft parenting, five percent to the child's efforts, and ninety percent is down to rich genetic endowment from granddad. Child development experts have no doubt, after much expensive independent research, arrived at the same conclusion. The evidence is overwhelming.

However, I have recently uncovered the possibility of a hitherto unsuspected (by me) factor when I read the report of an Ofsted inspection of the pre-school establishment attended by two of my grandchildren attended by two of my grandchildren, Saplings Nursery in Henham. Personally, I would have called it Sucklings, but there you are.

As you will know, there are many supervisory and regulatory organisations these days, Off-this and Off-that, which on the whole seem to be pretty self-serving. They provide well remunerated employment for the shy and timid, who in turn appoint their friends and relatives as "inspectors", or so I surmise; how else do you explain sending in retired police sergeants to assess hospital operating theatres and part time teachers to look at police stations. But I digress.

Ofsted, having gone through a number of sticky patches, seems to have got over itself if the report into Sucklings, a tip-top outfit, is anything to go by. Not a single spelling mistake and that's not just thanks to spellcheck – you can always tell; the homophones catch them out every time. These Johnnies can spell. The highest rating (Outstanding) in every category has been awarded to Sucklings. You will be happy to hear that they have abolished the old-style lowest rating (Satisfactory = Frankly, Pretty Awful) and substituted Inadequate, which gets you closer to the truth.

Much praise is heaped on this nursery: "children thrive in this nursery", "excellent levels of consistency and coherence between home and nursery", "the owner, manager and staff have high aspirations" – it goes on and on. The phrase that caught my attention and brought tears to these rheumy old eyes and warmed my heart, however, was "they effectively teach children how to identify and manage risks for themselves". No zero risk here, no dressing up their charges in goggles and full body armour before allowing them to pick up a conker before confiscating it. A good deed in a naughty world this place.

So, I have had to reappraise my allocation of credit for my grandchildren's astonishing development; 90% grandpa's genetic endowment, 5% infant effort and 5% skilled parenting no longer seems fair. Gramps still gets 90%, but parents, child and nursery each now get a 33.3% (recurring) of the balance. I now expect to receive a letter from Ofsted offering me a highly-paid job, with the reasonable prospect of an OBE in due course. I am ready to go.

If you want an honest account of a child's progress your best plan is to consult the grandfather, or an Ofsted inspector, of course. Grandmothers can be unreliable and parents are positively misleading. You hear some pretty dubious claims from parents: "fully toilet trained before she left the delivery room", "fluent speech, deploying a vocab of a thousand words after three months", "running errands to the shops at six months". Why, even my own daughter, an otherwise sensible young woman, tells me that my two year-old granddaughter, Maggie, is now speaking Danish. I once saw her point at a butter dish and say "Lurpak" and she likes a bacon sandwich, but that seems to be the extent of it. You get the idea.

So, if you live a long way from Striplings my advice is that you move house and make friends with Linda Davies – the capo de tutti capi down Henham way.

Brid's many and varied pleasures and treasures

Over the past six months or so I have been renewing my acquaintance with Bridlington, a place that was familiar to me during my childhood. It was to Bridlington that my mother and brother were evacuated during the Second World War. The family who took them in, Mr and Mrs Daddy, went into the B&B business after the war and we all stayed with them for a week every year for our holidays – "us holidays" as I used to say before grammar school education straightened me out, or bent me out of shape depending on your point of view.

As a child I was interested only in sitting on the sand and visiting candy floss stalls on the front. There is much more to Brid than that, as I am now discovering; the Old Town, for example. Although there are here, as everywhere, empty shops, some of which are rather dilapidated and decaying, the area has great charm still, with a family butcher, greengrocer, baker, several interesting restaurants and a lively craft gallery. I may be wrong, but I assume that this is a conservation area in which case I believe that the local council has powers to enforce restoration.

The Old Town has received some publicity recently following the filming there of parts of the new Dad's Army production which, after the film is released, will probably increase visitor numbers. A bit of sprucing up seems in order. Once a thriving business district with banks (now closed, but one in use as a beauty parlour) which it will never be again, this quarter could be a thriving tourist destination. Would Lottery money be available? In view of the many outlandish causes to which the Fund awards grants it is hard to judge the likelihood of such finance. At the very least it should be given conservation are a status and carefully looked after by the local authority.

The East Riding has a wealth of Grade I listed churches, among them the well-known Beverley Minster and St Mary's in that town, but the lesser known Bridlington Priory is a real gem. It is a thriving parish church and a local landmark, but also of architecturally and historically it is of great interest. Dating back to the time when the religious houses in Yorkshire owned much of the land, providing employment and food on a large scale, this Augustinian foundation was, before Thomas Cromwell took an interest, extremely wealthy. I have no childhood recollection of even seeing this building – too interested in rock pools and beach cricket, I suppose – but it is well worth a visit.

For those, like me, whose tastes are rather lower brow, the local fish and chip shops are an obvious destination. After many years of bitter exile in the South where chippies of only the inferior variety are available, and in America where fish and chips are frankly disgusting and haddock unheard of, my return to Yorkshire was my chance to catch up for lost time. Bridlington is blessed with many excellent fish and chip shops. My favourites are the one in Main Street, Sewerby, which is only a few paces from the house where I stay when in the area (sadly, open only from March to September), and 149 on Marton Road. 149 is the only chippie where you don't have to ask, in a shame-faced way, if batter scraps are available, they are routinely offered. Five star joints, these.

There is, of course, a price to pay for scoffing all that deep-fried haddock – those lipids won't lower themselves – and that is exercise. Where better to do that than the beach between Bridlington and Sewerby, and what better company than a pair of enthusiastic water dogs. But only last week I had an amber warning: the seal I had excitedly spotted off-shore turned out to be one of my own dogs that had ventured further out than I had realised. A sign of ageing, perhaps.

Possibly, but not to worry. We now have, thanks to North Yorkshire County Council, an "older people's champion" whose brief is to look out for those of riper years, particularly if they are lonely or, like me, deluded. Our champion and others like her located elsewhere are urging that GPs should be required to offer "social prescriptions" (whatever they may be), a proposal that will warm the hearts of medical practitioners everywhere.

I often feel lonely myself when Mrs Croft is watching endless re-runs of cookery shows on the telly. I shall be asking my GP to prescribe NHS funding of my membership of the Old Malton Wine Tasting Club. He may, however, detect a conflict of clinical imperatives here. We shall see.

Rollicking good read about hacking scandal

If, like me, you followed the phone hacking scandal in which the now defunct News of the World newspaper and other tabloids were implicated, and grew confused, weary, and even drowsy as it dragged on, you may be interested a book I have just read. It is Dial M for Murdoch, by Tom Watson and Martin Hickman. It was published in 2012 by Allen Lane, the Penguin Press, but I had not heard of it until a few days ago; I read it at two sittings. I acquired it for a song from a bargain bookshop.

Any confusion you may have felt is understandable. There were several operations being conducted by the police, mainly the Metropolitan Police Service but also the Devon and Cornwall Constabulary. These were Operations Caryatid (intrusion into Royal voicemails), Elveden (police corruption), Glade (illegal use of the Police National Computer), Motorman (breaches of Data Protection Act), Tuleta (computer hacking) and Weeting ('phone hacking).

There were plenty of villains in this story: newspaper reporters and private detectives hired by them breaking the law, vindictive behaviour towards innocent people that destroyed lives and broke up families, and officials willing to be corrupted by ready money. These included, among others, police and prison officers, and armed services personnel. But there were also heroes: Tom Watson, MP for West Bromwich and his co-author, Martin Hickman, a journalist on the Independent newspaper, and two Manchester solicitors, Charlotte Harris and Mark Lewis.

Some of the institutions whose sole purpose it is to protect the public were found wanting: the Metropolitan Police, the Crown Prosecution Service, and the Press Complaints Commission not least among them. They come across as self-serving, pusillanimous and incompetent. At a time when there was evidence in their possession that the private detective, Glenn Mulcaire, who was instructed by News International staff, had a list of over 4,000 names of individuals whom he was "targeting" and it was clear that he had "hacked" over 800, the Met was maintaining that victims were likely to be in low double figures, though in this they were not helped by a bizarre legal ruling by the DPP (later reversed). When the actress Sienna Miller, a truly courageous young woman, asked the police if her name was on Mulcaire's list it took eight months to reply. Foot-dragging and obfuscation was everywhere, and in the meantime people like Ms Miller were left to suspect their entirely innocent family members and friends. The leadership one expects to find in these organisations appeared to have been replaced by self-serving managers.

There were moments of high farce that would have not looked out of place in a Tom Sharpe novel. A Member of Parliament, a former clergyman, who had displeased News International, found that a photograph of him dressed only in his underpants had been posted on Gaydar, a gay social networking site.

The Commissioner of the Metropolitan Police accepted a £13,000 freebie at a health spa, an error of judgement that cost him his job and would have been instantly seen as such by any rookie bobby on his first day on the beat. For 20 years a News of the World crime reporter also acted as an interpreter for the Met during interviews of Ukrainian suspects, and was himself later arrested.

No fewer than 10 staff in the Met's Public Affairs Department were former employees of the News of the World.

Cash payments were being made, sometimes breathtaking amounts of money, to informers, retained contractors and officials. It is not mentioned anywhere in the book, but one wonders if Her Majesty's Customs and Revenue troubled to pursue the recipients of these dodgy payments for tax owed.

Book jacket blurbs are not always reliable, but this certainly is. I quote: "This book is full of details which have never been disclosed before, including smears and threats against politicians, journalists and lawyers. It reveals the existence of brave insiders who pointed those pursuing the investigation towards pieces of secret information that cracked open the case ... You will hardly believe it."

Exactly so. A rollicking good read, if a depressing one.

Family gravestone will need a 'Please Turn Over'

Easter was a splendid family occasion, which is just the way I like it. Ten of us round the table for Sunday lunch with me in poll position to intercept the untrusting glances and to hear (new batteries in the hearing aids, of course) the barbed remarks that so often enliven such gatherings. On this occasion the pleasure of savouring the sly looks of envy as Mrs Croft offered a described the many advanced features of her fine new motor car. I do love family life.

Lunch was followed by a disconcertingly large invasion of children of all ages who had joined us to celebrate the first birthday of grandson, Oscar. I had spent some time during the preceding days coaching him to say "granddad". This was the first word uttered by his sister, Maggie (2), and I had been hoping for a repeat performance from young Oscar, but the little blighter has been proving resistant. I doubt if the tuition will continue in my absence.

Other aspirations will come to the fore.

Young Oscar seemed rather underwhelmed by his many gifts, especially mine – a collection of Thomas the Tank Engine books and a rather natty little outfit I picked up for a song at Tiny Tots in Finkle Street. My original plan was to get in early with a Swiss Army knife, but his mother vetoed this. I have noticed that the older I get the more supervisory she becomes, but I don't say anything.

Her daughter, Maggie, has inherited this irritating trait. I had been enjoying a bit of a kick about on the lawn with my senior grandson, Archie, when she marched up, gathered the football into her arms and headed off towards the house saying, "What do you two think you are doing?" Archie, who is eight and perfectly able to put a two-year-old in her place (I've seen him do it), asked her if we could have our ball back so that we could continue to our game. She gave him an incredulous look, said "Well....No" and toddled off like a self-important school prefect. We meekly followed and helped ourselves to another chocolate egg. From her collection.

The weekend also featured a grand wedding feast, that of a friend of my daughter, Carol Bishop, whom I have known since she was a rather unprepossessing eleven-year-old who turned into a geneticist, now an accountant. It started at five and finished at midnight – so I am told, I was long gone by then. It was a fine evening with excellent food, prepared by Small Aubergine, and incomprehensible music of the loud variety, but the highlight for me was when I was dragged off by two very attractive young Asian women, who clearly know a good thing when they see it, and forced into a three-seater photo booth to be snapped in fancy dress, a sort of triple selfie. I thought I was being kidnapped. Don't laugh – it could happen.

Anyway, during all the family talk I heard that there is these days much controversy, post-mortem, about the wording to go on the parental gravestone. Wanting none of that, I decided that I should stipulate the matter myself. This is what I have come up with:

Here Lies
Howard Croft
Publisher, Obedient Husband
Stern Father and Doting Grandfather
Unreliable Friend to the Unwary
Bachelor of Arts and Queen's Scout
And All Round Good Egg
In Abraham's Bosom at Last.

And below that, in the fullness of time and in a smaller typeface obviously:

Also his Relict
Mrs Croft

When I showed her this draft Mrs Croft went a bit quiet, possibly because of the brevity of her entry. Space is an issue of course, but I did point out that the back of the stone could be treated as a continuation sheet in the event that anyone comes up with anything worth adding. I think it will be fine.

Watch this space when election purdah ends...

A prominent member of our local community, whom I shall not name, has pointed out to me that my tendency to write about personal and family matters does not cater to the interests of readers of this newspaper. He cited, for example, weddings and birthday parties, Mrs Croft's foibles, my own enthusiasm for consumption of wine and other things which I can no longer recall. His criticism, delivered in a caring way, makes a fair point. I shall mend my ways and in future try to focus on matters of more importance.

I am slightly hampered at the moment by the rules of "purdah", which prevent me from touching on anything that is in any way political until the great democratic process of May 7 is completed. I have to say that the idea that anything I might say could swing the voters is, to say the least, fanciful and grotesque. However, it is for this reason that I have recently confined myself to my plans for the inscription on my tombstone, the antics of colander-wearing religious zealots and similar trivia.

For now, we are still in purdah. In my time as a publisher great care was taken over the selection of titles for books in the interests of both clarity and non-duplication.

One wit reversed this principle: Alan Coren, the humourist, published a book with the title Golfing for Cats. I no longer have a copy, but if my memory serves the cover illustration was of a cat in plus fours swinging a golf club and wearing a swastika armband. Although the book contained nothing about golf, cats or the Third Reich he chose this title because he had discovered that books on these topics were invariably hot-sellers. This strategy, he thought, would ensure record sales by appealing to keen buyers in three markets and oblige booksellers to buy three copies, one for each section of the shop. The book did very well.

Too much thought can be given, however. Two I remember. A distinguished medical man, an expert on addiction, proposed taking a number of academic articles and cobbling them together into a book with the title Drug Scenes. We were at a loss to know quite what he had in mind and I was despatched to investigate. So, off I toddled to explore the thinking of the great man. It immediately became clear that "scenes" was a word he was keen to deploy in the title – I suspect he had been eavesdropping on his teenaged grandchildren.

Anyway, quick as a flash I asked him to whom his book would be addressed. To the readers of The Sun newspaper, he firmly replied. I pointed out to him that statistically Sun readers were unlikely to go into bookshops. "Nevertheless", he insisted, "they will buy this one if we sell it in newsagents' shops." I doubted this. "My dear chap, the readers of The Sun are very worried about their children and drugs. They talk of little else at dinner parties!" Of course the book was published with a cover, designed by his granddaughter, depicting a silhouette of a street person, head back and with a bottle raised to his lips. Looked like George Melly blowing his horn, but even so it did not do well at the tills.

I was also involved in publishing, on behalf of the Nuffield Foundation, a book of medical and social issues surrounding old age, an important topic I am sure you will agree, and we worked happily together on it.

However, they, the Foundation, insisted on giving the book the title Dependent Territory. I was uneasy about this; it is an apt term for old age, but not one in general use, not even among geriatricians.

I mentioned my misgivings, but I was not persuasive. A clever title, they said; too clever by half I thought, but did not say. Following publication I found a copy in a bookshop shelved under Colonial History. Ah, my prophetic soul! Another dud.

Only another couple of weeks and purdah will end. Two smoking barrels and loaded for bear, that'll be me. Details of the renewal of my "subscription" to the brown bin and, if I can get what I already know from a non-confidential source, other dark doings. Hold that thought.

Politically correct? No, just silly

Bizarre reports in the press, so bizarre that they are hard to credit, that the World Health Organisation (WHO), which has noticed that some diseases have names that are unflattering to some and offensive to others, is urging that we re-examine things. It draws attention to "swine flu", "bird 'flu", "Spanish flu", "monkey pox", "Cook's disease", "German measles" and "Legionnaire's disease" to make its point.

Those diseases whose names are associated with animals might, it is said, lead to unnecessary culling of such animals – pigs, for example, in the case of swine flu. Those associated with places may have an adverse effect on tourism, Spain, say, though why the WHO feels that it should be concerning itself with the income of tourist destinations is hard to fathom. Spain does not seem to have suffered in this respect since the influenza epidemic that occurred almost a hundred years ago.

Cook's disease may cause offence to people working in the catering industry, says WHO, but I doubt that there is any evidence of this. Does Marco Pierre White suffer from low self-esteem because of the name of an inherited condition first identified in a family called Cook? I don't think so.

Where will it end? The press reports put it down to "political correctness gone mad", a phenomenon much loved by journalists, but I put it down to silliness at the WHO, whose staff clearly haven't enough to do with their time. There was no mention of what was once widely known as the Italian disease (syphilis) and here as the French disease (which is fair comment). The French tried to get it known as the English disease, but it never caught on for obvious reasons – lack of originality being one of them.

Beyond the medical sphere, to which the WHO thankfully confines itself, there is scope for other things to worry about. Chinese burns, a primitive form of torture once in vogue in school playgrounds I remember, and Russian Roulette, a popular parlour game in that country, should both be eradicated because of the negative connotations. We are luckier here: English rose, English oak, full English breakfast, English humour are all positive and should not be banned. Scotch mist, on the other hand ...

On the home front, Mrs Croft has attended her third of four one-day courses at the Malton Cookery School, this one on Italian cooking, hosted by Georgio Alessio, the proprietor and chef of the Lanterna Ristorante in Scarborough, which I understand enjoys a considerable reputation. I had the presence of mind to pop in before the course commenced, and ahead of Mrs Croft's arrival to urge the chef not to encourage her to buy a pasta machine. These are expensive items bought in a rush of blood to the head and destined seldom if ever to be used, rather in the way that electric sandwich toasters are supplied by parents to all those eager new undergraduate students who don't use them, and if they do don't clean them. My little visit seems to have done the trick.

I must say, though, that the cookery school is responsible for a definite improvement on the catering front at our house and I am looking forward to trying some gnocchi sometime soon. Mr Alessio must have been somewhat taken aback to be told by Mrs C that she knew a thing or two about this Italian specialty having watched The Godfather III film several times. It can be a risky thing to mention to an Italian chef that you have found culinary inspiration in a mafia-inspired film.

He seems to have taken it in good part, but, who knows, when next he appears in Malton he may be carrying a violin case.

We have promised to visit his restaurant; perhaps I shall show up there with a violin case of my own and find out how he feels about my little joke.

I believe the Cookery School is planning a one-day course on knife sharpening and butchery skills. I may go along to that and show off my knowledge acquired from watching Donnie Brasco, another mafia entertainment.

'Fowl' debate over name

The organisation for ethical treatment of animals (PETA), which has done so much globally to influence thinking and legislation in respect of endangered species, seems to have lost its marbles. It is putting pressure on an eighth century public house in St Albans, Ye Olde Fighting Cocks, to change its name to Ye Olde Clever Cocks. The director of PETA is quoted as saying: "Changing the name would reflect today's rejection of needless violence and help celebrate chickens as the intelligent, sensitive and social animals they are."

Well, there you go. I would have thought that someone high up in an animal welfare organisation would have been aware, if only vaguely, of the difference between a chicken and a cockerel. She definitely missed a trick there in not knowing the difference – a valuable gender lesson on a plate, begging to be deployed. I do wonder whether she has ever met a chicken. I have never myself been on close terms with these birds, but I do know that when they are bored or feeling low they are inclined to peck each other to death – hence the term "pecking order". Not the behaviour I expect to find in sensitive, social creatures. Dolphins, say.

But she has a point and bully for her for making it. Cockfighting has been illegal in this country only since 1845 so it is possible that the message has not yet sunk in, especially in St Albans perhaps, since this pub was given its current name almost 40-years after abolition. Is PETA going to stop there, I wonder? The St Albans boozer may be uniquely named, I don't know, but there are plenty called The Dog and Duck and they are not, as far as I know, named in honour of local petting zoos. Horse and Hounds and Stag and Hounds are plentiful; the references are unmistakable and, I assume, deplored by PETA. They are going to have their hands full firing off sanctimonious letters to publicans all over the country. My fear is that they will have to divert resources from attending to the interests of tigers and elephants in order to meet the challenges of this important new work.

Other special interest groups may want to learn a thing or two from PETA in promoting their own agendas going forward. Vegans, for instance, might well think it worthwhile to press for name changes of pubs called The Cow or The Lamb, and I think I once came across one called The Barnsley Chop, in Barnsley possibly. Disgusting. In the High Street in Hull, just along from the Wilberforce Museum, there is an excellent watering hole called The Black Boy, so named because it was on these premises that African slaves were auctioned in the days before Wilberforce and his cronies did their work. Scope here for those interested in the promotion of racial harmony.

We are fortunate in our locality not to have pub signs and names that reflect shameful pastimes and practices of days gone by, but there are two, both Royal Oaks, that show a singular lack of respect. They were named, I understand, mockingly to commemorate a Prince of the Royal Blood who was more than usually wooden – I hesitate to name him. "Well-carved, but wooden" they said of him. Should these all be changed to The Prince Charming?

I am no more an historian than I am a moral philosopher, as you may have spotted, but I do think that we should think twice before airbrushing out parts of our history, as PETA seems to want to do. But if they insist on deleting references to cock fighting I think they could come up with something better than Ye Olde Clever Cocks, especially since fowl have never enjoyed much of a reputation for intellectual prowess. What about Ye Olde Curried Chicken in recognition of the multicultural society in which we now live? I think PETA need to return to the drawing board. Thinking twice before speaking would be a good start if they do not wasn't to appear to be foolish in the press.

I remember the famous occasion when the Princess Ferguson complained over dinner to Denis Thatcher about the unwelcome press coverage that embarrassed her every day. "Have you ever", he said, "Considered the possibility of keeping your mouth shut?" Good advice.

Observational day out at Bempton bird sanctuary

I have revisited Bempton after a gap of, I guess, fifty years. The basis has not changed; thousands of sea birds kicking up a racket and making a dreadful mess on the cliffs. I like to think that I'm as shallow as the next person and sure enough, I found myself wondering how much you would have to spend on All Purpose Flash to do a bit of a clean-up. I am my mother's son.

However, what has changed it that the Royal Society for the Protection of Birds has transformed the site with a new visitor centre, cleverly designed (and safe) viewing platforms with provision for wheelchair users and walkways making access easy throughout the site. You have to pay to get in now, of course, but the price is reasonable; no OAP concession, I couldn't help noticing. At no time were we approached by RSPB volunteers to sign up to make a donation; no chuggers.

Our fellow bird watchers, apart from a couple of school parties, looked to be on the dark side of sixty and were much of a type. They were all dressed in brightly coloured anoraks, lots of them in jaunty bobble hats and quite a few were wearing those "shorts" that stop mid-calf with pockets down the sides for compasses, glucose tablets, heart medication and, who knows, forbidden herbs possibly. All the requirements of a grey army on the move. Socks and sandals much in evidence.

With one exception, all were skinny, brown and bright as buttons, and they emitted that air of self-satisfaction that comes with making it as far as retirement and the knowledge that back at home there is a cupboard filled with Ordinance Survey maps for every location apart from Bempton. That map was hanging round their necks from a nifty cord and wrapped in cling film in case it rains. It wouldn't do to ask, but I would not be surprised if their bedtime reading is OS maps of the Lake District.

The exception, who creeped me out, was younger, overweight and scowling. He was dressed top to toe in army-style desert camouflage and was tough looking. Even his binoculars were camouflaged, and they were by far the largest pair I saw that day. Goodness knows what he was carrying in his combat pouches. I was put in mind of that chap who made a name for himself in Hungerford and I was careful not to catch his eye.

Mrs Croft and I must have stood out in this crowd; I didn't look like a sniper, she didn't look like an off-duty Girls Guides mistress. She was decked-out in a multi-coloured fisherman's smock, picked up for a trifle in a Dartmouth chandlery, with a handy pouch for her mace spray, and boating shoes. She looked every inch an admiral's daughter gone trendy. Myself, I have never been accused of being at the cutting edge of fashion, until recently. I did a bit of painting in my best jeans and messed them up a bit; washing did not improve them, so I took a blue marker pen and touched up the white paint. A chemical reaction must have taken place because ragged holes appeared, some affording a tantalising glimpse of manly thigh. This, then, was me at Bempton and as you would expect I attracted many admirers, some of them women. I had no need of the red bobble hat so popular among bird watchers during the mating season.

But, to graver matters. You may have heard that Andrew Pitt, inky fingered scribe on this newspaper, is leaving for greener pastures, which is a pity. Andrew it was who, four years ago, approached me with the suggestion that I might like to write a monthly column in his paper. I did like and I agreed on condition that it be weekly – an obvious case of an old man in a hurry. Ever since, he has been my handler and not a word has he changed in that time, nor an offering spiked. I shall miss him.

Who will be my new handler, I ask myself. Not, I hope, some jumped-up intern in a Primark suit, with a brand new blue pencil in his (or her) eager fist and ideas about managing freelance hacks. I am lying awake at night thinking the worst. But at least I won't have to listen to Andrew saying every time we meet, "You were nothing when I found you".

A return to this folly would be very foolish

As you have no doubt read in the news pages, the judicial review outcome was a comprehensive denunciation of Ryedale District Council's decision to grant itself planning permission to enter into a deal with a developer (GMI Holbeck) to build a supermarket on Wentworth Street car park. Four of the five grounds on which it was alleged that the decision was unlawful were upheld; only one was needed for the decision to be overruled. Costs were awarded, yet again, against the Council.

I have read Mr Justice Dove's arguments, conclusions and judgement and you might like to do the same, although I warn you that it is not an easy read, filled as it is with legalisms and unfamiliar acronyms, but it is damning. Apart from rehearsing and analysing legal precedents, much of the focus is on the planning officer's report to the planning committee recommending the second grant of approval for the superstore on the car park, which was duly given.

The report, together with supporting documentation, was circulated prior to the planning meeting; not included was the Inspector's Report in which the first grant of approval was overturned. That was given to members at the meeting itself. This, of course, is an old dodge. As the judge indicates, this is an important document that carries great weight.

The Inspector's report is, however, referred to in the planning officer's report. Of this the judge writes: "I am satisfied that the officer's report did mislead members, and mislead them significantly, as to the findings of the Inspector........." and, later, "As a result of the approach of the officer's report and the absence of analysing the impacts on the livestock market scheme the conclusions which they reached in relation to the planned investment were inchoate". A fine word, inchoate. Other, important aspects of the Inspector's Report were simply not referred to. This is a broad enough skirt behind which members can hide, as suspect they will.

Where does that leave us? The developer has applied for leave to appeal, so the saga may continue for some time yet, but I doubt that leave will be granted, so comprehensively was the Council criticised by the High Court judge. I am hopeful that the car park will remain just that for many years, for two reasons: the proposed addition of large numbers of houses in Malton and Norton will bring with it increased demand for parking, and the requirements of major local events, the weekend food events, the Ryedale Book Festival, cycling competitions and other projects in the planning stages, will see a growing need for special event parking capacity.

In the meantime, there will be a legacy of bitterness left by this sorry situation that will be very difficult to overcome, but that is for the future. What has been exposed by Mr Justice Dove is at best gross incompetence, at worst something else altogether. It is not in the nature of public sector institutions to clean the stables. We, the tax payers who will have to underwrite the many hundreds of thousands of pounds of unnecessary legal costs, have not been treated straightforwardly; the smiling assurances that the five million pounds was "never the issue" and that there was no operation of a party whip were not honest and known not to honest when they were given.

I predict that we shall see finger pointing within the Council, with councillors blaming officers and vice versa, and high level claims of ethical purity. No-one comes out of this well, but if I were a senior Council officer I would be reaching for a lawyer and trying to get my union representative to take an interest. For them, careers are in jeopardy, for members of the Council only loss of low grade political position, and not even that for four years.

I have said that I am hopeful that the car park will remain a car park, but I am not optimistic. The Yorkshire Post of Saturday 11th July (two days after the court ruling) carried the story under the headline "Judge puts block on village's store plan". (Village?)

In that report Ryedale District Council leader, Linda Cowling, is quoted as saying: (this ruling) "enables the application to be reconsidered by the planning committee at a later date".

I assume that this means that a third attempt will be made to give itself permission to do what it wants, that is a bit of nifty asset stripping. I am reminded of the Old Testament (Proverbs 26:11): "As a dog returneth to his vomit, so a fool returneth to his folly". Indeed.

Navigating the Derwent on hottest day of the year

I am not, as I may have confided to you before, a great fan of the summer; I do not worship the sun and, once Easter is out of the way, I begin to look forward to the days shortening again, a process that, thankfully, starts in June. However, there are some things to which I look forward, one of which is our annual evening boat trip up the Derwent. This year we enjoyed the hottest July day since the hockey stick curve first appeared on a climatologist's graph.

Riparian water rights, as far as they govern the use of Derwent, go back to those happy days when barons were still slitting each other's throats and plotting against the King; boating is forbidden, except to a tiny privileged few. One member of this elite happens to be a friend of ours and it is only because of his generosity that we are invited to put together a small party to motor from a secret mooring to Kirkham, along the way breaking out the victuals and uncorking a few bottles. We have in our time included in our crew a Prince of the Church, assorted lesser clergy, retired warriors from the armed forces and a few, like us, lesser mortals.

On previous occasions there has usually been an unseemly rush to demonstrate manly qualities, rather faded in some cases, by seizing the tiller – but not this year. No Grace Darlings this trip. In spite of my calls for volunteers, I was left alone at the helm, jaunty in a greasy Breton cap that may have been snatched from the body of bargee following a freak boating accident. I was able to navigate the many new obstructions created by the Environment Agency's wise and sensitive decision to lower the water level, since reversed.

I successfully negotiated the obstacles – many large trees and the occasional weekend cottage, which had slipped into the river as the banks, to the surprise on no-one, had collapsed.

As I had no help on the bridge there was little opportunity for to enjoy the picnic, managing only the occasional nibble and a cheese biscuit or two. It was in some ways a relief. I watched as my crew wolfed down cold roasted quail, baby quail they looked to be, provided by an over-enthusiastic Mrs Croft. My inner vegetarian was crying out to me. I don't know what to do with these little birds, apart from feel sorry for them; do you crunch them whole like whitebait? I am not a fan of finger food in any case, much preferring to sit at a table, knife and fork in hand, bib secure. I was peckish when I got home that night and, I confess it, a little tipsy.

When we dropped anchor at Kirkham, the loveliest of spots, we were confronted by a large party of youngsters, aged from about five to sixteen by the look of them, cavorting on the banks. They were having a fine time. A couple of campfires were on the go from which drifted the unmistakeable aroma of sausages being cooked, the older children were swimming in the river and skulling about in inflatable canoes. The older girls were looking after the younger children, while to the older boys were leaping off the bridge and climbing trees to reach greater heights from which to jump into the water, admired by the older girls. I noticed that the daredevils were clearly assessing the risks, occasionally adjusting heights in the interests of safety, but no-one was ticking boxes. It was a real pleasure to watch children freely having a good time, taking a few risks, oblivious to the red backs and shoulders that would later give problems at bedtime. That is how it should be.

Anyway, that's enough about the mating rituals of young bloods letting off steam after finishing their exams, let's get back to me. I am not one to blow my own trumpet, in fact I don't even have a trumpet, but I fancy that I cut quite a dash on the river; manly arm relaxed and confident along the tiller, deftly keeping us course, wisps of greying barnet peeking out from under the old Breton number. You get the idea. I could hardly get over myself. And I was not alone; I even noticed Mrs Croft, chomping on the bones of well-done quail, shooting appreciative glances in my direction – not something I see every day. But now, back to reality and the keyboard – home is the sailor, home from the sea, crew all accounted for.

Ghoulish recollection after fancy dress party

We were invited to a party, to be held at an address in an otherwise respectable locality, with instructions to attend in fancy dress. Guests appearing not dressed up, the invitation made clear, would be stripped to their undies and kitted out from a play-box provided by the hosts.

This is the kind of invitation that, on the basis of a quick glance, I would normally decline, but in this case there were compelling reasons for accepting. The threat of being reduced to one's Kevin Klines, skinny Chinese coolie legs on show for the amusement of gaping strangers, brings a certain focus to the mind. I decided to wear a leather jacket and shortie-jackboots, exemplifying 1960s biker-chic. One ill-intentioned fellow guest muttered "Biggles Flies Undone", just loud enough for me to hear.

Mrs Croft borrowed an elaborate garment, a pink confection complete with tiara, from a grand lady, resident of Pickering, and passed herself off as Barbara Cartland possibly, or Lady Docker. Far too much slap I thought, but maybe that's just me.

Wigs were a big feature of the evening. And masks. I did wonder, as I stood in line for a burger at the barbeque, how many of those whose identities were so concealed were in fact vegetarians giving themselves an evening off, hoping to go unnoticed. One fellow in a mask, who had the look of a Londoner about him, engaged me in conversation, addressed me as Vera. I think he must have been MI5. You may remember that one of our less interesting spies, John Vassall, who was active in the fifties and jailed in the early sixties, was known in his irregular private life as Vera, when he was not lifting secret documents from Admiralty House. Was Mr MI5 on duty, hoping to flush a sly, traitorous fox from its coven, or did he have something else in mind?

It was an interesting do, but we did not stay late because my hearing aids, with fresh batteries inserted that very day, did not tolerate the increasingly loud music as the evening wore on. We slipped away. We must have presented an odd spectacle as we tottered home – a superannuated Sopwith Camel pilot unsteadily supporting a clearly tipsy Barbara Cartland.

Once home, I had trouble sleeping and once I got off I was troubled by weird dreams caused, I am sure, by the images I had retained of those guests who had chalked their faces white; deathly pale were they all. Maybe it's a new fashion. I did read recently that the Home Office now receives thirteen hundred applications a year for permission to exhume the bodies of departed loved ones. Only ten years ago the number of such applications was fewer than two hundred a year.

It has always been my understanding that such requests come from the police, who make them only with great reluctance and for very good and obvious reasons, usually with the agreements of families concerned. It now appears that families are cutting out the middle man and going directly to the Home Secretary. The reason most commonly given for these requests, which you may think rather ghoulish, is that people are moving house and want to take the dear departed with them, along with shrubs from the garden and all the light bulbs.

Are we seeing in this trend an upsurge of filial piety, or a commendable desire to keep the carbon footprint under control by reducing the need for long car journeys to visit graves and by so doing to save the planet? I have no idea what costs are involved in all this, but they must be considerable, especially as exhumations seem to be carried out under cover of darkness, which will involve double-time for the man, operative might be the correct term, on the back-hoe. More research is needed in the many departments of sociology scattered about the country.

How does the Home Secretary decide these cases? Is there here something like the Mann Act in the United States, under which it is a Federal offence to cross state lines "with sex in mind", whereby crossing county boundaries with a corpse on board is a crime unless there is consent from the Privy Council, say? I remember – this was many years ago – being driven from New York State to Connecticut by a rather serious chauffeur to whom I reported myself, insisting that I had indeed had sex in mind as we crossed the state line and inviting him to turn me in to the FBI.

What will happen to me, when I am happily tucked up in Old Malton cemetery, if my children are overcome by a piety I have so far not detected in them. One lives in Oxfordshire, the other in Essex.

Ludicrous rules of the BBC TV licence

Having contributed over two hundred articles for this column I have occasionally got a few facts wrong, or upset some people; it would be surprising if it were not so. Some boldly write spirited letters to the Editor rebuking me for my shortcomings, the local health visitors, who took issue with my views on vitamin D, are a good example, and they have the satisfaction of seeing their rebuttals printed in the paper. Others, notably those who dwell in the palaces of the mighty, are more craven and confine their boldness to marking their letters Not For Publication. What is the point of that?

There is one such palace where the nabobs are not so shy: the BBC. I have twice mocked the Beeb's determination, from its position very far behind the technological curve, to retain the television licence fee for its funding. On both occasions a letter was fired off. The more recent occasion was when I pointed out that pubs and restaurants without TVs, and therefore no licence, are at risk of criminal prosecution if customers watch broadcasts on their mobile devices while enjoying refreshment.

Not so, say the licensing authority. A customer in a TV-free public house, if he has a licence to view at his home address, may operate his tablet or whatever without exposing the licensee to penalties, but only – this is the bit I hadn't appreciated – *if he does so using a battery to power the device, but not if he plugs it into the mains.* If he uses a mains socket, or doesn't have a licence at home a criminal offence is being committed not by him, but by the pub landlord. The consequences are serious: a fine of a thousand pounds on conviction and a criminal record to go with it, with almost certain loss of his drinks licence and his livelihood.

The situation, as clarified by TV Licensing North, is more complicated and more ludicrous that I had thought at the time of writing. You may remember that I quoted from the Old Testament (the verse about dogs returning to their vomit, directed at Ryedale House) and you may have been surprised to find Biblical scholarship coming from such a source. This was no one-off I'll have you know. I have another, one for the licensing zealots: "Thine own mouth condemneth thee, and not I: yea, thine own lips testify against thee" (Job 15.6).

What is our poor pub landlord to do? Demand sight of a TV licence from anyone looking at the screen of a smart 'phone or a tablet and ban them if they fail to do so and in any event chase away anyone caught stealing his electricity, licensed or not? Most will cut their losses and buy a licence, but it cannot be right.

This is a ludicrous rule, smacking of a hastily applied Elastoplast in response to changing reality without regard for unintended consequences. Where, I wonder, do the railway companies stand in all this? Most provide electric sockets for us by passengers with mobile devices; does every carriage have to have a TV licence, or do ticket inspectors have to examine TV licences as well as travel documents? Have they been told?

Not quite exhausted from my Biblical research, I went to the TV Licence website to truffle about for more nonsense and I was not disappointed. If you are lucky enough to own a cottage by the sea, or a flat in Leeds, in addition to your main residence you are obliged to buy a second licence. However, if you own a static caravan you don't need one. What's the difference (apart from the price)? Before all you caravanners relax you should be aware that under no circumstances may you watch TV in both your home and your caravan *at the same time*.

Not only that, you are required by the licensing authority to fill in and return a silly form "certifying" that this will never happen. Alternatively, you could seek advice from your MP about the possibility of frequently "flipping" your main residence.

These rules are not only laughable and unjust, they are unenforceable and they bring the BBC into disrepute. I was at one time a member of a club one of whose rules prohibited "the repeated introduction of boring guests", on pain of expulsion. To which should have been added bureaucrats. As for me, I shall not be buying a TV licence for our flat in Leeds.

Council decision verges on economic loonacy

Those of you who are feeling bruised by our own district council's use of our money during the still ongoing Wentworth Street car park horror show, and appalled by the mismanagement involved may be cheered by the thought that there is always someone worse off than you. You are right.

The market town of Bishop's Stortford, Hertfordshire, where once I lived, has quite a story to tell and many of its features will be familiar. This town (population 38,000) is prosperous, has a thriving town centre with many independent traders and is "governed" by East Herts District Council (EHDC) most of whose members do not live in the town. In 2009 the council sold to a developer town centre land (including car parks) and buildings for £7,350,000, which was independently valued at the time at just under £10,000,000. This property was described by the Conservative leader district council, Cllr Linda Haysey as "an expensive white elephant, draining public resources". The developer was granted planning permission (by EHDC, of course) for a hundred-million-pound development – a controversial decision.

The people, and especially the local traders were not happy; there were protests, delays and a judicial review. Work on the development was originally scheduled to begin in 2012 and be completed in 2014. The developer has now withdrawn and the council has bought back what it sold for £7.35 million for a cool £19.5 million giving the developer a profit of over £12 million.

Cllr Haysey now says of this new deal that it is "a rare opportunity to purchase a major site that has a central role in the life of Bishop's Stortford and the rest of the district." The 2009 deal cannot be compared to the 2015 deal just announced, she said, because the council now owns not only what it owned six years ago on the cheap, but also Charrington House, valued in 2009 by the council at £1.4 million, and "three delightful cottages". So that's alright, then. According to my local source, there are indeed three cottages, but they would not be universally described as delightful and are worth considerably less than a million as a job lot. The white elephant had become a pearl beyond price.

My source for all this is the Herts and Essex Observer, a local paper that I regularly read all those years ago when I lived in the area, which has been fearlessly reporting this nightmare since 2009.

A local resident, a former banker who before his retirement oversaw the Queen's financial affairs, commented: "I am not sure what I find more startling: the sheer incompetence and lack of fiduciary prudence of the council or its supreme arrogance in trying to justify its actions. The national media and the Governor of the Bank of England are, justly, critical of 'Corbynomics'. The far left loony economics pale into obscurity compared to this example of idiocy."

Not reported in the press, as far as I know, was a meeting between local traders and the developer during which he assured them that the total loss of all-day car parking spaces that the development was to have involved was immaterial since shop proprietors and all their staff cycle to work. This was greeted with gales of laughter. He insisted, on the basis of no evidence, but based on "green" aspirations, that he was right. So, black is white and white is no colour at all, as my mother used to say. Anyway, if a white elephant can turn pink, what's the problem?

On the question of parking for workers, it is said that late in the negotiations it dawned on officers and staff of the council that the sale of the council owned car parks meant that their privileged free parking on them would no longer be enjoyed. A deal was, of course, done. Trebles all round.

So, we don't know how lucky we are, here in Ryedale. We are facing the prospect of our council buying back our car park for £15,000,000 from GMI Holbeck as we have not yet sold it. But, who knows what clauses lurk in the contract that might explain RDC's reluctance to contemplate the collapse of this ill-conceived project. The contract, of course, is more secret than the home address of the head of MI5. No rejoicing just yet. If catastrophe comes it will doubtless be declared to be a famous victory.

School choice should be automatic for siblings

When I was a child and approaching primary school age (infant schools they were then called) it was generally accepted policy that children with older siblings already enrolled were given priority for admission. This was still the case when, twenty-five or so years later in the late seventies, my own children started school. I do not recall any discussion about this; it was regarded as "a good thing" based on the belief that subsequent children would be more likely to settle in when siblings were already established.

Sometime later, exactly when I do not know, the policy changed. It was decided that giving priority to following siblings was "unfair" to other children and they had to join the pool for allocation of places by officers of the education authority. Some were lucky and joined their brothers/sisters, others were not. This was understandably unpopular with parents who were faced with, among other things, less convenient school trips, especially in rural areas where schools may be widely separated by miles or by long journey times.

Later, by a process of what might be called "authority creep" among council officers rather than policy change, it appeared that sibling priority was completely reversed and children were actively prevented from joining their siblings. I do not know if this philosophy was universally adopted, or what the justification for it was, but it seems to have been from press reports, widely applied and will probably be denied.

It was recently announced that central government has instructed education authorities to revert to the old policy of giving siblings automatic priority, one that was generally viewed as reasonable and humane. It will be interesting to hear the lengths to which officers will go to circumvent this in favour of their own preferred policy.

It seems likely that the timing the independent appeals procedure, in some areas at least, is designed to frustrate appeals, only three percent of which are upheld. This low success rate may owe something to the fact that appeals are heard throughout September into late October, by which time children are already enrolled in and attending classes at schools not of their parents' choice. Many appeals lodged during the summer term are likely to be abandoned. Given that the authorities know with certainty that there will be appeals it should be possible to so arrange matters so that all hearings are held before the start of the new school year. An earlier start, perhaps, or more trained tribunal members would be a start. Managing processes is what civil servants are supposed to be good at and one cannot but wonder if this is deliberate.

An appeal was lodged this year on behalf of a child in my family against a decision not to give her a place at the school where her older brother is established. The effect of this decision, apart from giving the child the comfort of attending the same school as her brother, was to place the two children in schools a considerable distance apart (this is in a rural area), put the family in a logistically impossible position in delivering the children to school and collecting them. It also involved the four-year old in unacceptably (according to the tribunal) long journey times.

The appeal was upheld. The tribunal's report, although expressed in the restrained language characteristic of such communications, was critical of the Admission Authority, agreed with the father's claim that it had not behaved properly.

Matters were even worse for the council officer who attended to tribunal to defend the original decision and to oppose the appeal. His own testimony, documents and calculations demonstrated to the tribunal's satisfaction that the decision could and should have be different, and the child admitted to the school of choice. The tribunal did not refer directly to it, but I am told by the father that the officer had difficulty handling the numbers involved, none being higher than thirty.

You can't help wondering where they find these people; is there a special college they all attend? On the national stage it is probably much the same, with the emphasis on process rather than outcome. Reading a book about Harold Wilson recently, I discovered that he had attempted in the sixties to reform the Whitehall civil service; the Humphrey Applebys were too much for him, and it came to nothing. Interestingly, it emerged at the time that the three divisions, Administrative, Executive and clerical consisted of an eye-watering 1400 staff grades. Imagine doing annual performance reviews in that environment.

Charity shop bargain buy and generational jargon

If you are married to a bit of spender, as I am, you will make your economies where you can. My strategy is wherever possible not to buy new, particularly in the clothing line. A few years ago I bought a fifty-year-old Crombie overcoat, in new condition, from Greyhound Antiques, for sixty quid. A new one would cost nearer a thousand these days, although you can find "crombie-style" items for much less, but they are mostly rubbish. Mine is the real thing and has attracted many admiring glances.

Only last week I was browsing in St Catherine's Hospice charity shop, a regular haunt of mine, and spotted a black winter coat that looked about my size – certainly my price, a snip at thirty-five pounds. It was a Burton's number, so practically an antique. I slipped it on, struck a few attitudes in front of the mirror, liked what I saw and handed over the cash.

This lucky find enabled me to get rid of a navy blue Yves St Laurent coat that I have had for over twenty years. I have never liked it and I don't suppose I have worn it on more than half a dozen occasions in all that time, in spite of the label, or possibly because of it. I took it to the charity shop and advised the volunteers, a cheerful lot with a surprising working knowledge of the Data Protection Act, that they should charge more for it than I had paid for the Burton's number.

Mrs Croft's reaction was odd, to say the least. You do realise, she said, that that's come off a dead person. I must say it hadn't occurred to me. Did she think I had been roaming a battlefield in the Napoleonic Wars, relieving French casualties of their decent threads? I pointed out to her that she off-loads plenty of her old clobber onto charity shops and I doubted that ladies are swanking about in it saying "Oh by the way, I got this off a dead woman". She went very quiet.

Rosie our flatcoat is now, after four weeks, half way through her post-operative recovery period and I am still head orthopaedic nurse; Mrs Croft is the Matron and Tessy, the younger dog, is the bad influence. We have had to cancel all our social commitments until the end of the year, parties, dinners, trips to London and so on. I have done a rough calculation and found that the resulting financial savings won't be far short of the fee the vet charged for the surgery. If the recovery period is prolonged, we could end up making a small profit. Already on the plus side I have been prevented by nursing duties from attending a wedding leaving Mrs Croft to represent us both. I suggested that we toss a coin to see who would be the lucky one, but the decision had already been made.

Brooding in the kitchen, watching a dog with a shaved leg, my mind turned to a minor misunderstanding between me, my daughter and my hearing aids. I had attended a wedding earlier this year and during the reception I had sloped out into the grounds to escape forced jollity that strangers indulge in on such occasions. There I found a youth, late teens I suppose, also skiving and moodily kicking a football about. We fell into conversation and wound up having a bit of a kick-about. In due course we were both dragged back in to listen to the speeches and I thought no more about it.

A few days later my daughter said, "you obviously made a big impression on Saira's nephew; when he heard you are my Dad he told me that he thought you are really thick". Nice. I was probably not at my best intellectually that day is how I defended myself. "No, not thick – sick. It's a compliment, apparently. Like "wicked" used to be." I remember that, and "well wicked" – high praise among the dermatologically challenged not so long ago. Cool!

I lack the self-confidence to deploy this newly acquired vocabulary, in fact generational jargon is dangerous territory. For me it always was – I was too self-conscious to say cool even when it was cool to do so. Sick, or what?

Scheme Ryedale council should take on board

This year's run up to Christmas, the bit I enjoy the most, has been somewhat marred by a convalescent dog requiring constant attention and an outbreak of winter vomiting disease in our house – no names, no pack drill whatever that means. Suffice it to say that she is now fully recovered.

My grandchild, Maggie, who is not spending Christmas with us this year, has got it into her head that I am on close personal terms with Father Christmas. I think that when I wrote to him (I had copied her in) to alert him to the fact that Maggie would not be here this year the warm terms in which I addressed him may have given this impression. The following exchange between her and her mother took place:

Maggie: Mummy, does granddad like Father Christmas?

Mummy: Yes, I think so. Everyone likes Father Christmas.

Maggie: Do granddad and Father Christmas sit downstairs drinking wine?

Mummy: Well, you had better ask granddad about that.

Maggie: I think granddad likes wine.

Mummy: Ah, well.......

I have just received the Winter Issue of the East Riding of Yorkshire Council newsletter, Bridlington and Driffield edition. It is a well- produced four colour affair, 32-pages of useful and interesting information without the self-serving PR character of the old North Yorkshire Times publication that very few miss, I imagine. It is a lively read, surrenders its meaning readily and appears to be an in-house publication with, if that be the case, surprisingly high production values. Ryedale District Council should consider it a model – look and learn.

Two services provided by the East Riding Council stood out as excellent community services. Free parking is being provided in all council-run car parks and on-street parking locations for the three weekends running up to Christmas, a very welcome contribution to Christmas that local traders will no doubt appreciate. Normal parking rules will still apply, such as time limits and parking bays designated for disabled motorists. I am sure that small traders in Malton, Norton, Pickering and Kirkbymoorside would welcome such support from their council during this busy trading period. Next year, perhaps?

Secondly, there is concern in the East Riding about bogus taxi and private hire drivers who surface particularly during the Christmas period when demand is high. These drivers have not been vetted, their vehicles have not been passed as safe by the council, and they may not be properly insured. In the interests of public safety, the council will be putting taxi marshals at the taxi ranks in Bridlington and Beverley between Friday 18th December and Saturday 2nd January.

They will be on duty from midnight to 3am with a brief to ensure that there are orderly queues, people have enough money for the fare home and to ensure that they are not getting into rogue vehicles. This will be the fourth year of the operation of this scheme. Ryedale council, please note. I am sure that your colleagues in the East Riding would be glad to help with advice. If so, I wonder who the Ryedale marshals would be. Not Council officers, those princes who like to disappear promptly at five and who in any case would be reluctant to perform such duties, whatever the hour, without a police escort. Councillors, possibly? A few potential bouncers there, even among the men. We'll never know – too imaginative a scheme, which would in any event be ruled out by a robust three hundred and sixty-degree risk assessment exercise involving all stakeholders.

This is the final appearance of my column this year, but I shall be back DV on the 6th of January after a two week break during which my grandchildren will come in like lions and when they have gone I shall retire to a darkened room like a lamb. I have very much appreciated your kind and helpful comments when our paths have crossed over the past twelve months. I hope that you all have a very happy Christmas, followed by a year of good health and happiness and possibly a sprinkling of lottery wins.

2016

RSPCA frowns upon 'novelty dog attire'

I hope that you all enjoyed your Christmas and New Year break. I certainly did. One of the many highlights was a visit to Audley End, a stately home near Saffron Walden, for a ride on the steam railway Santa Special with two of my grandchildren, Maggie and Oscar. It is miniature steam railway not life-size like our much envied North Yorkshire Moors Railway, but the event was organised with careful attention to detail. We met Father Christmas, of course, who was accompanied by many prancing elves, and every child received a gift and a few words from the man himself.

However, it was not all fun and games. There were puddings to be stirred, gifts to be wrapped, dogs to be wormed – the usual chores – in preparation for invasion by another brace of grandchildren, Archie and Imogen.

Speaking of dogs, the RSPCA, mindful of its reputation management problems I'm sure, has sprung into action on their behalf. The practice of dressing up dogs in what is known as "novelty dog attire" is, says the RSPCA, unacceptable. During the festive season dressing up dogs as Father Christmas is apparently a popular way of including pets in the celebrations, but this will not do says Dr Gaines (doctor of what is not disclosed) and may render them unable to express their feelings.

If your dog is old, young, sick or has a particularly sparse coat (she has Bedlingtons in mind I suspect) you may put it in a dog coat, a sort of matinee jacket specially designed for them and permitted by the RSPCA. Otherwise, your mutt must go au naturel. If you stray outside these guidelines and trick out your best friend as an elf or a Christmas tree fairy, watch out. The RSPCA is only too ready to prosecute you.

You may think that it is cute to attach to your dog bow ties, ribbons, ankle warmers, Halloween costumes (available from all good pet shops), but it is not, it is a crime. You can be sure that there is an RSPCA inspector, or one of his snouts, living near you. This is not the same thing as a police inspector, but the fact that they wear almost identical uniforms suggests that that the RSPCA doesn't mind a bit of confusion in this area.

I am a reasonably experienced dog owner, "owner" being a term frowned upon by the RSPCA but its use is not, yet, a criminal offence, and I have never felt tempted to dress my dogs up. In my view dogs look better without adornment, but I don't much mind if others indulge themselves. I have never seen a dog looking distressed when dressed, but I am not a "doctor" of course. Professor Gaines has attempted to disguise her prosecutorial enthusiasm behind a wholly unconvincing assertion that she does not want to come across as "a party pooper......or as the fashion police, either". Warm and fuzzy she is not.

So, if you come to grief and find yourself banged up in a cell for the night for titivating your terrier, don't say I didn't warn you. Your best plan will be to plead insanity.

As we do not know what new offences the RSPCA might come up with in its attempt to rehabilitate itself you should take care in other areas. If you have an Alsatian, speak to it only in German and avoid mentioning the war, if you have a Scottish terrier on no account hum the National Anthem and under no circumstances sing verse 6 in which Marshal Wade is urged to crush the rebellious Scots. Failure to follow this advice could be deemed by "doctors" as liable to lead to canine psychiatric damage, possibly psychosis.

Taxpayers still suffering the pain of car park saga

The Wentworth Street Car Park saga continues, like a grumbling appendix, giving pain and crying out for surgical intervention, but who will wield the knife? A couple of young Turks on the Council (Duncan and Ives) seem willing, but they have yet to find the key to the operating theatre. Who is suffering the pain? Well, you and me for a start, the tax payers. Consider the following.

According to figures supplied by Ryedale District Council (RDC) in response to a Freedom of Information request, Council costs on this project to date amount to an eye-watering one million six hundred and ninety thousand plus change (£1,690,000+). Or, mouth-watering if you are banking the cheques rather than issuing them. There are broadly four categories of expenditure: legal costs, consultants' fees, relocation expenses and the purchase of Harrison House, that posh office block by the station.

Legal costs, so far, amount to £391,736. This figure includes £150,000 incurred by the Fitzwilliam Estate in a court action against RDC. The Council lost the case and the court ordered it to pay the other side's legal costs and this is the amount that the Estate is claiming. The award is not in dispute, but the amount is and the two parties are negotiating; if they cannot agree it will go back to the court and an order as to the amount will be made there. Either way, those lawyers will be upgrading their BMWs I am sure.

Consultants' fees, again so far, stand at £15,500 This, to my untutored eye, is a surprisingly modest amount, but, in view of the current state of play one may be forgiven for wondering if this was value for money. A consultant, for those of you who do not know, is a chap wearing two-tone shoes who, when he follows you through a revolving door, comes out the other side ahead of you. You know the type, easily distinguishable from lawyers, who seldom wear two-tone shoes.

Relocation, has racked up £51,627, presumably a final figure. This is the cost of winkling out the occupants of the site the Council is hoping to sell to the developer for the now truly legendary amount of five million. These were the Citizens' Advice Bureau (£9,151), Coast and Vale (£2,476) and the Boy Scouts (£40,000). "I promise to do my best" are, as every boy scout knows, the opening words of the Boy Scout promise (mission statement I suppose we would now say) and they certainly seem to have lived up to their values on this occasion. As a former Boy Scout myself, I am proud of them, but I do wish that my money had not been involved.

Harrison House, the smart office accommodation adjacent to Malton railway station, was purchased for £868,898 and subsequent refurbishment clocked up a further £344,926, giving a total of one million two hundred and thirteen thousand eight hundred and twenty-four pounds (£1,213,824). I have no idea if the price paid was reasonable, but as the Council is not experienced at property investment, nor should it be, it seems unlikely that it would come out on top in negotiations with a commercially experienced organisation. On the other hand, this building is recognised locally as the best, most modern office space in the town, so who knows?

This does, however, raise questions about the huge sum spent on refurbishment, approximately 40% of the original purchase price. Possibly money was spent on making it fully accessible to disabled people – lifts can be expensive I know, but even so. In the meantime, part of the property is rented out to a charity. If it has to be re-sold, and it might come to that, I would be astonished if the whole cost, including refurbishment, were to be recouped.

So, where next? It seems that the Council, or the ruling party, is determined to press ahead regardless and that they have the support of the senior executives, or so I hear. It is proposing to renew the contract with GMI Holbeck, the developer involved, not for a limited period as was once understood, but for a significant number of years. In view of the judicial reversals and the stupefying expenditure, this is surprising. One assumes that it has the support of the Head of Finance and the legal officer – also surprising.

One wonders what the new 2015 intake of councillors, even the Conservative ones, make of all this. Do they really find comfort in the thought that there is still enough of the five million pounds (not yet in the bank and unlikely to be that much anyway) will be enough to justify such a decision?

As for me, I'm polishing my two-tone shoes.

Wentworth Street car park – saga finally ends

Just when we thought it would never end – it did. At the meeting of Ryedale District Council on Thursday 13th January the leader threw in the towel and supported a motion to abandon the ill-conceived ambition to see a Tesco built on Wentworth Street car park. This outcome came as no great surprise – it had been pre-announced to the press the day before – but the meeting was not without interest, drama and, thank goodness, a bit of comedy. There was a full house. The public gallery was packed and every councillor was present, except one who had been prevented from attending by a fall of snow that afternoon, reminding me of the time John Major's problems with his wisdom tooth prevented his presence in London when another Conservative leader found herself at the end of her tether.

All the usual suspects spoke up. Councillor Lindsay Burr, obviously unwell and confessing to be deaf in one ear, had risen from her sick bed to be with us. She scolded the blue phalanx across the chamber in her characteristic manner and showed due respect to Councillor Cowling by referring to her as "our supreme leader". Quite right. It was Councillor Burr, of course, who had, along with Councillor Paul Andrews, kept alive the flame of resistance on the council.

Councillor Andrews appeared rather stunned to find himself on the winning side of this particular debate, but managed to get over all his points in spite of looking like a man who had just emerged from a long period in the wilderness. Councillor John Clark, as ever disguised as an Old Testament prophet, Elijah possibly, was on top form and made a silent point by remaining seated during opening prayers using the time to pour himself a hot drink from his Thermos. He niftily put together on the hoof an amendment to an amendment, which unfortunately was not passed.

An astonishing bravura performance was put on by Councillor

Keane Duncan, a young man barely out of his teens. He together with Councillor Luke Ives had been largely instrumental in bringing us to the happy outcome at the end of the evening, I assume by talking some sense into their Conservative colleagues. He put their motion with considerable aplomb for all the world as if he had been on the council for a decade. He received a warm and obviously genuine tribute from Councillor Clark, a man not easily moved to praise a Tory.

The Conservative bench maintained complete silence throughout the meeting, all wearing serious faces; were they sulking or just glum? It was impossible to tell. The exception, of course, was Councillor Linda Cowling. Cllr Clark's amendment (which was not passed) to her amendment (which was) would have required her to apologise to us all and she did refer to this. What she is sorry about, she said, was the cost of mounting legal defences – I think I caught her glowering at the Fitzwilliam Estate's representative, Mr Roddy Bushell. To be sure, the Estate's legal challenges did come at a cost to the council, but had the council behaved lawfully a lot of expense and trouble could have been saved all round.

And what of the Moaning Minnies of Malton? They threw their sweaty nightcaps in the air as their spokeswoman, Emma Brooksbank, stood up generously to praise the sterling efforts of those in the community who had worked so long and so hard to resist the council's loony plan. In truth, she herself did most, but she was too shy to mention it.

I hope that I shall have no need again to type the words Wentworth and street, but I am not optimistic about that. There was no hint of contrition in Cllr Cowling's words or manner, and she spoke of exploring other opportunities to develop the "underutilised asset", as she terms the car park. It did not sound as if leaving it as a car park is likely to be considered, in spite of the plans for extensive house-building in Malton and Norton.

In the meantime, I am looking forward to using the car park, at least the parts that do not flood.

Floods highlight stupid acts on and off road

Compared with many other communities in the north and in Scotland we got off pretty lightly when the flooding visited us after Christmas. This year, again, we saw the best of which people are capable and the worst. The staff from the Environment Agency worked tirelessly to pump away the water that had closed Town Street in Old Malton, supported as usual by the fire service.

Unfortunately, in spite of "road closed" signs, many motorists came racing along Town Street to be confronted by deep flood water. The more timid turned round and went back, but the arrogant few ploughed on into the water at high speed making life for the emergency service workers more difficult than it needed to be. I witnessed one being stopped by an Environment Agency worker and asked, "what part of 'road closed' do you not understand?" He was told to turn round and go back and loftily replied that, if he thought he could get through, he was entitled to try. A small crowd gathered and he discovered that we did not share this view and, tail-pipe between his Range Rover's wheels, away he scuttled.

Worse than these individual acts of stupidity and selfishness was the corporate incompetence at the top of the Environment Agency. These suits in their dry offices do not serve us well, nor are their staff on the ground well led. Their decision, effectively to allow the Foss to flood into York, will no doubt be the subject of an enquiry and so too, I hope, will be the revelation that the pumps at that site were not accurately calibrated. Lessons, no doubt we shall hear, have been learnt, but these will merely be words.

More fundamental a problem is the Agency's determination to allow rivers and other water courses to return to some prelapsarian state in the interests of wildlife. They implement this policy by refusing to accept that failure to dredge is causing flooding – the only cause they recognise is global warming. There are many causes, including, of course, their own failure to take sensible, practical measures. It was a great mistake to marginalise the drainage engineers in favour of the bird watchers and rare newt fanciers who now run things. That clock will take some turning back.

Against this background of environmental challenges there was good news in the family. Many years ago I gave my then very young nephew, Michael, a mixed bag of old coins, farthings, pennies, florins (remember them) and half crowns. How I came by them I cannot now remember, but I thought they might amuse him and I certainly remember hoping that he would not swallow them or push them up his nose the way children like to do. That child is now a man, a junior doctor in fact, part of whose job it now is to remove foreign objects from the nostrils of enterprising small boys. Why is it always boys?

Anyway, he came to stay just before Christmas and told me that he had been researching these coins and had discovered that one of them has a value of one thousand pounds. I thought I had given him some scrap metal and now I find that I am helping to pay off his student loan, at least that is what I hope is happening. I have always regarded him as lucky blighter – tall, good looking if you like that kind of thing, good grades at school, a place at medical school, attractive fiancée, all that kind of thing – and now he has discovered a dud coin is worth a mint. I shall be asking him to buy my lottery tickets "going forward", but he may think of me as that uncle who was too mean to buy me a decent birthday present all those years ago and refuse to help me out.

Good news on the journalism front; I have discovered that many of my articles were reprinted during 2015 by a dozen or so localpapers. So, wherever in this region fine minds congregate to consider and savour quality prose, there will you find my name mentioned. Remember, you read it all first here in *The Malton and Pickering Mercury*. How my old English master, Mr Roberts, would gape in astonishment and disbelief.

Radical thoughts to brighten up winter

What a strange place the world has become. An Oxford college is considering air-brushing Cecil Rhodes out of history by removing a statue of him because a student (a former Rhodes scholar no less) feels insulted when he walks past this statue on his way to sit his exams.

The Archbishop of Canterbury is proposing to muck about with the dating of Easter in the interests of schoolteachers, who get fatigued in years when Easter falls very early and also very late, and holiday tour operators in early ones.

The Chief Medical Officer, Dame Sally Davies, has reduced the maximum permitted dose of alcohol to 14 units and declared that there is no safe dose. Booze is out.

You may think that this is plenty for us to be going on with. I don't think it goes anywhere near far enough, but it is certainly a good start. There are many things that we could expunge from history as well as Rhodes, a rogue of the first sort.

Take chimneys. In my view we should compulsorily remove chimneys from all houses: they are a painful reminder to any sensitive soul passing them of the dark days when innocent small boys were sent up them to dislodge soot. How Father Christmas will cope and what we might do with our television aerials I cannot say, but solutions will have to be found.

Also, all traces of Henry VIII will have to be removed – he was, after all, a serial adulterer and wife-killer, any mention of whom will cause distress to all women. Holbein is out.

An attempt was made many centuries ago to fix the date of Easter, but abandoned as too difficult and has never been revisited by the

Princes of the Church. Until now. Our man Justin Welby is made of sterner stuff and it looks like he might pull it off, but he should be more ambitious.

Christmas might usefully be moved to July to avoid the risk of the bad weather that interferes with all our travel plans during the holiday period and would avoid that awful busy shopping period in December. It would please Santa, too, as there will be no open fires to singe his beard when he visits, although under my plan there won't be chimneys anyway. Lent too could be moved and placed after Christmas – a period of fasting would be so much easier after all the feasting on turkey and pies.

Now, what about Dame Sally Davies's plan to cut off our supplies of alcohol? She has told us that drinking wine, beer and spirits is the cause of many ailments including, but not limited to, heart disease, all cancers, neurological disorders, especially dementia, piles, halitosis and vibration white-finger (those cold cocktail shakers). She does not mention the odd epidemic of bed-wetting in the Wolverhampton area that I keep hearing about and she may be right; in my view it is almost certainly caused by global warming. That and Derbyshire neck, also not mentioned.

Archbishop Welby might like to lend a hand with this. Only last week in church the second lesson was the account of the miracle performed at the wedding feast when water was turned into wine, not just any old wine, but good stuff. This passage should never again be read in church, reminding us as it does of the pleasure of wine bibbing.

A suitable substitute might be the Old Testament passage: "Look not upon the wine when it is red. At the last it biteth like a serpent and stingeth like an adder. Thine eyes shall behold strange women, And thine heart shall utter perverse things." (Proverbs Chapter 23, verse 31). Indeed! Short, but punchy. Alternatively, references to wine could be removed and camomile tea substituted.

These are just a few of my ideas, all of which came to me over a bottle of Argentinian red – I'm working on my stocks to run them down before the new law comes in. I can't abide waste. Another, but it would require planning permission, not easily achieved even by an archbishop, is to change the name of the village in West Sussex, currently known as Hurstpierpoint. It is a painful reminder of the dark age when our public hangman was called Albert Pierpoint, known locally as "String 'em up Albie".

These are just a few thoughts to brighten up your new year. Cheers.

Judge's ruling may help to end heartless scheme

I hope that the recent ruling from a judge that applying the so-called bedroom tax to families with handicapped children and vulnerable adults is discriminatory and unlawful will ultimately lead to the collapse of this scheme. As you may remember, this inhumane tax, strictly a reduction in benefits, is applied to any family with "too many" bedrooms (that is, a spare room), and it applies only to families living in social housing (council and housing association dwellings), not owner occupied homes. No surprise there.

It is astonishing that it took judicial intervention to establish that a family with a chronically sick child whose needs include, for example, a room to store medical apparatus or to accommodate an overnight carer should not be penalised for having a spare room, which is hardly 'spare'.

Those of us who are lucky enough to have extra accommodation know its value in terms of putting up visiting family members, adult children and, more enticing, grandchildren. And also lucky enough to own our homes and not to depend on state benefits. Much is made of the 'right to family life' set out in the European Convention on Human Rights and this surely must cover a reasonable expectation of family members to visit and stay.

I know that my own life would be significantly impoverished without visits to and from children and grandchildren, even though I do have the daily presence of Mrs Croft whose company, guidance on which television programmes I would most benefit from and general supervision are indescribably valuable.

You can be sure that the politicians and officials who came up with this heartless scheme, and who apply it so inflexibly, do not themselves suffer from it. I have no doubt that our charming Prime Minister, the tireless 'Dave', has a room where he can lay out his electric train set and leave it ready for his use at any time. So also for that nice Mr Clegg over there in Sheffield with his extensive Lego collection; his finger prints are also on this legislation.

However, should the housing shortage become a national crisis, which is certainly possible, there is nothing to stop the government applying the principle to home owners through the income tax system in an attempt to drive us all into one bedroom hovels to make room for others whose needs are greater.

This is not a time to relax. I do wonder, though, if there are enough one-bedroom homes to go round, or even if anyone knows. Some people seem to think they have insight into the housing stock. You may recall the case of the family, living in a three-bedroom house and wishing to create a fourth bedroom in the roof space to accommodate an additional child. They were refused planning permission by officials on the grounds that their plan would 'reduce the number of three-bedroom houses' in the area. So there you are – someone in authority is looking after us.

It occurs to me to wonder what the definition is of social housing. It must surely cover any accommodation that is provided, in whole or in part, by the state. Number Ten Downing Street, for example, would qualify, as would all those MPs' second homes that we the tax payers so generously provide. I have no doubt that public officials in Whitehall and elsewhere will, if they are contemplating extending the penalties to the well-off that currently apply only to the less-well-off, will be up all night devising exemptions for their masters – and of course for themselves.

Speaking of public officials, I encountered a few at a meeting in December to discuss the longstanding and pressing problems of air quality at 'butcher corner' in Malton, and flooding in Ryedale. I must say they looked jolly pleased with themselves. These problems go back many years and not much has been done, or so it seems. Not so, we were told. Many reports have been written, one a 'final' report – but not really a final report because it is judged that the data it includes are now out of date and the exercise must be repeated.

It struck me, listening to the self-serving complacency at that meeting (held in the Malton and Norton Rugby Club, but the bar was closed) that these officials see their jobs as preparing and writing reports – not getting things done. What we saw as failure – floods and a continuing pong in central Malton – they saw as success. All those reports! So, now you know.

Strange language of professional jargon

During the ongoing dispute between the Secretary of State for Health and junior doctors my sympathies have been with the doctors. One reason is, and here I have to declare an interest, that my nephew, of whom I am very fond, is a junior doctor and the other is that the Secretary of State is such an unattractive fellow. And not very bright; taking on these young doctors is a high-risk strategy, especially as they are solidly united.

He does not seem to have grasped that NHS hospitals already run seven days a week, and that weekend admissions are in the nature of things pretty serious and should not be compared to routine admission Monday to Friday. My family has had recent dealings with a couple of hospitals. My sister was in the Royal Liverpool Hospital for a month in the autumn where she was frequently trolleyed down to the MRI scanner on a Sunday. His attempts to get GPs to work seven days a week came to grief during the pilot tests because patients didn't show up at weekends. Better things to do, I suppose; gardening is very popular and, who knows, relaxing in the arms of catamites.

I have spent quite a bit of time hanging about in York Hospital recently, where everything went very smoothly and promptly. We are getting used to the strange language changes everywhere: train passengers are now customers, an old 'improvement', and patients are service users. I suspect the latter term comes from managers, not doctors and nurses. I doubt if doctors, arriving at their clinics, ask the nurses "How many service users are on my list today, sister?"

A more sinister change in vocabulary is that service users are no longer discharged, but released – a term more commonly associated with prisoners coming to the end of their sentences. I was surprised therefore to notice in York Hospital a door marked Discharge Lounge. What can this be? Is this a room to which you are sent to relax if you have an unpleasant discharge?

Reading a patient information leaflet, I spotted another change: instructions on what to do when you come to the end of your course of treatment used instead the term 'your treatment pathway'. I would have thought that after the considerable adverse publicity given to the Liverpool Pathway, a long walk on a short pier to you and me, the word pathway would have been best avoided. Even where they still follow the now discredited Liverpool Pathway (it has still its devotees) the name has been changed.

I wrote to the York service users' department and suggested that that they avoid professional jargon in such leaflets and also mentioned that it would be useful if it were to carry some guidance about likely charges levied in the hospital car park. They replied, but not to the jargon point, only to the car park charges. It's all on their website, apparently. Posting information on a website is the first resort of the idle and unconcerned who want to tick the box marked 'tell the public'. Some people do not go online, and in any case navigating many websites is, perhaps intentionally, difficult.

However, what is very handy, and it doesn't matter if not everyone uses it, the click-and-choose feature whereby you can go online and make your hospital appointment yourself, though you don't hear much about it now. The traditional system of hospital administrators allocating a slot for you and writing to tell you about it is a bit hit and miss. You can of course ring them and request an alternative, but it is all very wasteful of time and money.

Naturally, we are all very excited by the prospect of popping along to a hospital and meeting a doctor, but we do have other things to do and some commitments cannot be set aside at the drop of a hat in order to enjoy such a treat. I have in mind, for example, funerals, leg-waxing appointments and important sporting fixtures on the telly, Wimbledon especially. Click-and-choose makes life easier, although there is seldom any choice. Sometimes between York and Scarborough hospitals, which as we all know is no choice at all.

In the meantime, young doctors coming to the end of their two-year post-graduate training jobs are not applying for jobs in specialist training posts. Instead unprecedented numbers are seeking certificates from the GMC that will enable them to work overseas. Australia is the destination of choice. At £350,000 a pop to train a doctor to this point it is something we ought to avoid.

Alarming nonsense from medical chief

The office of Chief Medical Officer (CMO) is one that is rightly held in high regard and much coveted, in part because it brings with it an award, also much coveted among doctors, of a knighthood or a damehood – if that is a word. During my time as a medical publisher I met three of these distinguished personages, liked them very much and admired their forthright advice to their political masters.

The current CMO, Dame Sally Davies, is rather different, not least in being a woman, and the first. Also, she arrived in the office with her Dame Commander of the British Empire already safely tucked away in her Gladstone bag along with her fellowship of the Royal Society (FRS), the latter an honour granted to comparatively few medics, an honour not to be sniffed at.

All the more surprising, then, that she has, in the words of Dr James Le Fanu, a newspaper columnist like myself, 'plumbed the depths of anxiety-mongering scientific fatuity' by suggesting that women, when contemplating a glass of wine, should consider the possibility that such reckless behaviour might increase their risk of developing breast cancer. Has she forgotten the principle taught to all medical students: First do no harm?

GPs across the country must be rolling their eyes in despair and disbelief at this unhelpful intervention in the perfectly sensible 'reduce your intake of booze' campaign, which I fully support. I occasionally accept a small sherry at Christenings and, more rarely, a glass of port and lemon on Christmas day, I am only too aware that I may be over-doing it.

As a distinguished scientist and medical researcher, Dame Sally must surely be aware of the importance of distinguishing between association and causation. Associations are easy to establish – causation is trickier. I remember the publication a few years ago that revealed that tall men are, statistically speaking, more likely than short men to develop cancer of the prostate. It was, of course, bound to come out one way or the other and it was almost certainly what we men of science (and women, too, Dame Sally – don't run away with the idea that I am a sexist moron) call a statistical artefact.

But even if it were not, what can be done about it? When this finding was picked up by the popular press I noticed that many of my tall friends were looking drawn and uneasy, as were some of their wives, although a few I have to say looked uncharacteristically cheerful. My advice to them all was to persuade an orthopaedic surgeon to chop a few inches out of their shins, sufficient to put them into the lower risk category. None as far as I am aware followed up on this, though a few adopted an unattractive crouch when walking about, hoping, I suppose, that God would not notice and let them slip under the wire as a shorty.

I am sure that, if you looked hard enough, you would find all kinds of curious associations. Perhaps people with ginger hair are statistically more likely to be troubled by piles, those with 'O' Level Latin to suffer from Derbyshire neck, women with more than one child to get in-growing toenails – the list could go on. I am reminded of my daughter's health visitor darkly warning her that insufficient intake of vitamin D has an 'unclear' link to paediatric leukaemia. We have enough to worry about without this sort of alarming nonsense, especially when it comes from the CMO.

To all you ladies reading this I say this: worry by all means about breast cancer, it's natural enough, but you don't need to do it when you are uncorking a bottle. Even though I am short I worry about prostate cancer, but only when I am standing on a box or up a ladder. I do not give this advice lightly – remember, it's a little-known fact, men also get breast cancer, but it is not the odd glass of wine it is just rotten luck. Stay lucky.

Things to consider about the Great Referendum

So, the Great Referendum is upon us. Are we approaching a precipice or a gentle slope of the sunlit uplands? I expect that you are as bewildered by the advice of the experts as you are terrified by the doom-laden threats from both sides. Luckily, I am here to guide you.

I will, if I may, take you back to the early sixties when I was what was then known as a sixth-former and the hot topics in the debating society were hanging, very popular at the time, world hunger, and – the Common Market. In an attempt to focus the immature minds in his charges the then headmaster, Mr J. Leslie Nightingale, offered a series of prizes by school year for the best essays.

I am sorry to say that I did not win a prize, but Mr Nightingale did, at morning assembly, read out passages from my essay as striking examples of the kind of xenophobia and general shallow thinking of which he most disapproved. I had set out my fears of unforeseen (except by me) consequences of joining the Common Market. There would be, I suggested, hordes of Breton peasants piling through the Channel ports and pedalling into the Home Counties on bicycles loaded down with strings of stinking onions.

Worse, we would be invaded by smooth talking Italian ice-cream vendors, who would mask their sinister and disgusting intentions towards our womenfolk behind heavily accented charm. Frenchmen would follow to embezzle our savings and steal the best jobs claiming, every one of them, to be counts and dukes and skilful lovers. There was good reason why syphilis was known, then as now, as the French disease and I made no bones about pointing all this out. It was to be many years before we actually joined The Six, by which time my stark warnings had been forgotten.

Now here we are, looking at the possibility of getting out and there is much to think about. Do we want to be part of an organisation that spends grotesque amounts of our money in such a way that its accounts have not once been signed off by its auditors for almost twenty years? If the EU were a company all the directors would have been sent to prison long ago.

Shuttling between two seats of government, Strasbourg and Brussels – an unnecessary expense estimated at £500 million a year – the Commissioners make themselves useful by passing ludicrous legislation, mostly favourable to the French, but of little value to the rest of us. Only recently, they decreed that fishing with a rod and line off Bridlington beach for sea bass would attract a fine of £5,000, all in the interests of conservation of fish stocks. In the meantime, continental boats are bobbing about off-shore sucking up the very tasty items that Bridlington Man fancies for his supper.

Those who wish to remain IN seem remarkably laid back. This is because they remember when the French and Irish people held east referenda and voted not to ratify an objectionable treaty the EU Commission ordered them to re-run the votes to secure a different result, more in line with its own wishes and those of the Germans. That could happen here if, as we must suppose, our spineless politicians go along with it. Then would be a good time to apply for EU funding, also known as bribes, as the Irish will tell you.

Of course, leaving the EU, if we are allowed to do so, would not solve all our problems. We would still have crooked politicians fiddling their expenses and useless officials messing things up, but at least they would be our crooks, whom we could punish at the ballot box, and our incompetents who could be sacked, in theory anyway. Do not suppose from all this that I am anti-immigration. I am well aware that the influx of Ugandan Asians fleeing Idi Amin's reign of terror led to a rash of successful start-up businesses. I know from personal experience that the sudden arrival of a host of Polish plumbers in London improved things no end. And, not least, those European Jews who arrived at the London docks having been told by their shippers (people traffickers we say now) that this was New York, but they stayed anyway. Their contribution was to the ranks of doctors, lawyers, politicians and bespoke tailors. In the end it is about numbers – and the stink of onions, of course.

Afterword

During my career as an academic publisher I put the names of many professional men and women onto the covers of books, in the process helping to further their careers and, in some cases, fattening their wallets. Never in all that time, not even in my most psychotic moments of self-admiration, did I ever think that my own name would appear on a book.

It is true that as a schoolboy I entertained an ambition to be a journalist, my newspapers of choice being the then *Manchester Guardian*, now of course *The Guardian*, and *The Yorkshire Post*. These papers were the most distinguished regional titles in the country, both were provided in my school library and both I read every day. *The Yorkshire Post* had an additional attraction: its then editor was Sir Linton Andrews who had also been a pupil at my school, the Hull Grammar School. If he could do it, why not me?

I knew, of course, that getting into either of these papers from a standing start would not be possible, and I looked for a first foot onto the ladder – Linton Andrews himself, after all, once worked on the *Leeds Mercury*. In due course the *Hull Daily Mail* announced a vacancy for a cub reporter, and I was all over that opportunity like a cheap suit. But, there was another candidate: a fellow pupil whose father happened to be the Detective Chief Superintendent in charge of the CID in Hull and, inevitably, my rival got the job. This was my introduction to the way the establishment works. As it happens, this senior policeman was in the same class at school as my father, but my father, a lorry driver, was not a Rotarian, but moved in different circles

So that was that. His journalistic career took off – he moved on to the *Daily Express*, then as now not an especially distinguished newspaper, and he would have gone further had he not died of a rare disease in his thirties. So off I went to university, narrowly avoiding ordination into the Church of England (they, too, rejected me), and drifted into publishing where I busied myself nurturing authors and putting their names on book covers. And avoiding rare diseases.

In due course, in my retirement, got what I had coveted in 1962 when I was invited to write a weekly column in the *Malton and Pickering Mercury* – without pay, of course. To my astonishment and that of those who know me well, this arrangement has continued for five years. It is my good fortune that the redoubtable Mrs Croft is also a publisher and a more talented one than me, as she loses no opportunity to point out to me, and she is was who came up with the wheeze of this anthology – Howard Croft's Greatest Hits. She has knocked the thing into shape, badgered me into co-operating with the process and, I don't doubt, making the lives of the designer and printer a misery. For this I am grateful, unlike the designer (Helen Lowdell) and the printer (Nathan Best), both of whom will be on tranquilising medication for some time.

I never met Sir Linton Andrews, but I was there to listen to him when he came to the school as a guest speaker at our speech day and prize giving event. I remember nothing of what he said – it was, after all, over fifty years ago – but I do clearly recall what someone else said. The chairman of the school governors was Alderman Teskey-King, known to us boys, with that spirited wit that only schoolboys can manage, as Testicle-King. Also on the platform was an Alderman Boddy, possibly representing the City Council. But possibly not; he was, in addition to being an Alderman, also a funeral director and given the great age of most of the dignitaries present he may have been there in his professional capacity.

Be that as it may, it was Testicle-King's duty that day to introduce the guest speaker. Which he did with the following words: "What I alus say, 'eadmaster, is there's nowt better for an 'ealthy body (Boddy – geddit?) than a good dose of Andrews". The awfulness of the pun and the crassness of the sentiment wrapped up in it provoked a terrible groan from the eight hundred boys in front of him. This, we knew, was the kind of joke that only local councillors can manage. Linton Andrews did not respond to this ghastly quip.

Acknowledgements

I am grateful to the following, without whose help my column would not have seen the light of day and this volume would not have been possible:

Andrew Pitt, sometime hack at the *Malton and Pickering Mercury*, whose idea Howard's Way was and midwife to the grizzly infant. Ed Asquith, Editor of the newspaper, who has been supportive throughout and shown remarkable equanimity during tricky moments. Helen Lowdell, designer of Malton, for her professional work on all aspects of the design of this book. Nathan Best of Best Print & Design for his wise advice during the development of this project and his workmanlike skill in seeing it through the press, evidence of which you now hold in your hands. Sarah Tyson, without whom there would be no Ryedale Book Festival, for agreeing, along with her fellow trustees, to publication under the Festival's imprint. Deirdre Buchanan, a loyal reader and critical friend from the start who was kind enough to write the foreword to this volume. Ryedale District Council whose antics have provided so much copy over the years. Philippa Aldrich, who first got me started by asking me to write a blog for her start-up company's website in 2010: www.thefutureperfectcompany.com. Well worth a visit. Long term family friend Saira Hamilton for her great advice on self-publishing.

My son, Edward, daughter Helen Christensen, their respective spouses, Anna and Søren and my grandchildren Archie, Imogen, Maggie and Oscar who have not only enriched my life but provided much entertaining copy.

Finally, and by no means least, to my wife Fiona, known to most of you as Mrs Croft, for her quiet (usually) forbearance when I have, over the years, portrayed her in a bizarre and unflattering manner in my weekly despatches from Old Malton. She has done most of the work on this publication. Creating order out of my chaotic archiving system was no mean feat.

About the author

Howard Croft was born and brought up in East Hull, with his twin sister, Denise, and his older brother Peter; he attended Hull Grammar School. He studied Theology at Bristol University, and trained as a teacher at Manchester University before starting his career as Head of Divinity at Oldbury Grammar School in Worcestershire. His publishing career began with The Longman Group, commissioning educational works, both from his UK base and during 5 years of overseas postings in Longman Zimbabwe and Longman Nigeria.

Returning to the UK Howard moved into medical publishing – his specialty until his retirement - with one of Longman's (then) imprints, Churchill Livingstone. He moved on to become Publications Director of Gower Medical Publishing, and then to a long-term role as Publishing Director at the Royal Society of Medicine in London. Subsequently he worked with Blackwell Science as Director of Medical Communications, and with a start up online decision support service for doctors, now known as *FirstConsult*, which was acquired by Elsevier in 2000. So Howard moved to the America for 5 years in various leadership roles at Elsevier Health in Philadelphia. On return to the UK from this assignment in 2006, he moved from Notting Hill Gate to North Yorkshire. He continued a long-standing consultancy with the Royal College of Psychiatrists, and began writing a regular blog called *About Retirement* for the Future Perfect Company: it was this work that attracted the attention of Andrew Pitt at The *Mercury*.

Howard lives in Old Malton with his wife Fiona, and his two flat coated retrievers, Rosie and Tessy. He has two children, Edward and Helen, and four grandchildren, Archie, Imogen, Maggie and Oscar. And a granddog, Rufus.

About the Ryedale Book Festival

RYEDALE
BOOK FESTIVAL

Ryedale Book Festival is a not-for-profit organisation, made up of a team of friendly, dedicated volunteers who organise quality book-related events in Ryedale, North Yorkshire. Their aim is to create vibrant, affordable and inspiring events for everyone who enjoys reading, listening to stories, illustrated books and the spoken word.

www.ryedalebookfestival.com